Work by Thomas F. Cook

Novels
Blooming
Illyria
Miss Over

Plays
A Score of Zero In Tennis
Victoria's Children
The Chicken Screamer
The Cigar Tree
Lost Dogs
The gAy List
The Day Job
Like Being In Love
Side Effects
A Tendency To Say Ummm
The Names Have Been Changed

Other Works
The Family Of Charles Abby Cook

Forthcoming
Impaired, a novel.
The Cigar Tree, a novel.
People I Don't Talk To Anymore: tales.

A Score Of Zero In Tennis

By

Thomas F. Cook

A Score Of Zero In Tennis
Copyright © 1986 Thomas F. Cook
First published in 2016

All rights reserved.

◇ **C** ◇

ISBN-13: 978-0-9907206-5-2
ISBN-10: 0990720659

"When one is young one doesn't feel part of it yet, the human condition; one does things because they are not for good; everything is a rehearsal. To be repeated at lib, to be put right when the curtain gets up in earnest. One day you know that the curtain was up all the time. That was the performance."

Sybille Bedford -
A Compass Error

Acknowledgments:

This play was performed with the title "What's Mrs. Potato Head Doing On The Piano?" at The Pearl Theatre over two nights in the summer of 1986.

The producer was Pentatone Productions, later renamed Penta Productions. The director was Bruce Carmel. Stage management was by Deborah Samm. The cast was Kathy Levitan, Lorraine Wochna, Joyce Paton, and Karen Giordano. A fifth woman played the part of Joanne, but regrettably, I cannot find her name.

An explanatory note::

Between 1982 and 1986 I wrote about six plays, none of
which exist anymore. They were called *The Mouse, Past
Tension, The Sunroom, The Eviction, Change In The Gutter*
and a couple of others whose titles I've forgotten. They were
learning experiences and all bad. This play was the first time
I had ever attempted to write specifically for someone else:
in this case, a group of five women who had formed an
acting company, the stated purpose of which was to "create
interesting parts for women." They later staged a successful
two week staged adaptation of *The Yellow Wallpaper,* by
Charlotte Perkins Gilman.

This is as much their play as mine, as it was read and
rewritten and re-read and re-written according to what each
wanted for the part they played. Dialogue was tailored to the
way they spoke themselves – they were from different parts
of the country – and their input and insight into the
characters was important. I think it took more than a year of
sitting around an East village living room and reading it over
and over until they felt it was ready. Each character,
however, (and I'm completely guessing about this) ended up
hitting a little too close to home. It was too sarcastic and
illogical, although the audiences seemed to like it. In the end
the group more or less rejected it, saying they didn't like
what it said about women. I rewrote it one more time, sent it
out, and got some very positive response from various
theatres, including the Public Theatre and Manhattan
Theatre Club. MTC also sent it to an agent, who signed me
for a couple of years until nothing came of her efforts.

Pulling it out almost thirty years later to put it somewhere
more permanent than a box in my cupboard, I discovered I
had to rewrite only a few things here and there, until about
the last twenty minutes of the play. Those pages needed an

enormous amount of rewriting and the discarding of entire sections. Thus, up until the part where they dance to *Mr. Sandman*, the play is almost the same as what was performed. After that scene, it is almost a new piece.

I've come to think of this play as camp; something that is a caricature — not of women, but of psychology, self help and the verbal garbage of some forms of theatre. Oddly, the person who became the stage manager was the only one who understood that this was a campy piece.

I changed the name because I had too many negative responses to the potato head name.

✳

CHARACTERS

EMILY. 28. (*plays Cynthia*) Shy and quiet. Probably not meant to be an actor but hasn't realized it yet.

ANTHEA. 27. (*plays Zandilla*) A nervous and damaged person who intensely dislikes confrontation. But she has energy and is, in fact, an actor.

MIRIAM. 28. (*plays Beth*) A challenging and purposely offensive person. There is something unspoken between Rachel and her. They may have once had an affair, probably in high school. Rachel can't stand Miriam's cynicism. Miriam can't stand Rachel's positivism.

JOANNE. 25. (*plays Jeannie Marie*) A flamboyant and artificial person; a narcissist before narcissism became popular; completely devoid of empathy.

RACHEL. 29. (*plays The Silent One*) An overly serious person who is not attempting to be closeted about her sexuality, but is not forthcoming about it either. Miriam is the only one who ever refers to the author of the play as Rachel's "lover."

There are also several voices which are heard on a tape recording. One is the unnamed author of the play that they are rehearsing. The other are two high school friends of Rachel's, named Tod and Amy.

THE PLACE

A rehearsal space in New York City, East Village.

THE TIME

Act One. A Saturday morning in fall.
Act Two. A few minutes before the end of Act One.

Note: There was smoking in this play, because it wasn't
   an issue back then, but those spots can be skipped
   without too much trouble. I've bracketed and bolded
   the areas which can easily be eliminated to avoid
   smoking issues.

Additionally, one of the "gags" was that Rachel had
   a tape player and a large box of cassettes, which had
   somehow gotten all jumbled and mislabeled. In any
   modern production, this would have to become a
   cell phone and a portable speaker, and in the
   unknowable future, might be an entirely different
   technology. Whatever is used, I think it could
   probably be acted out with the same mistakes and
   gaffes. To adjust, I've written that she "looks for the
   song," or variations of that which just means she
   turns to her device.

A SCORE OF ZERO IN TENNIS

ACT ONE

(At rise: A bare stage or rehearsal space with a few chairs and a table. Emily enters carrying coffee, muffins, bagels and spreads for breakfast. She sets them down on the table, looks directly at the audience, and talks to the audience as she moves the table and chairs to the correct position. She is a calm, thoughtful person.)

Emily. I was in a play last fall. A friend of a friend of an acquaintance asked me to be in it — she was directing — and being an actress and never having acted since college and college being in the middle of Iowa where no one lives anyway and being close to thirty and getting scared I'd never get work and wanting more than just about anything to feel like I had more in my life than typing, I practically hit the ceiling when she asked me. I was so excited and at my first rehearsal Rachel, the director, gave me the script and I grinned and smiled even as she told me that I had the part with three lines. I had twenty three words. And even though I was happy to be in a play, there was a part of me that was terribly disappointed. But I didn't say anything. I shut my mouth and decided to make my part live in spite of its small size and the somewhat confusing script. I was the first replacement Rachel needed. Miriam was the sixth. It was that day that I decided that my small part was a mixed blessing. It gave me the opportunity to watch and notice the things during what I call the fateful "Miriam rehearsal" that nobody else seemed to. (Anthea *enters loaded with bags and everything.* Anthea is a very nervous person and does not like confrontation.) There were five of us. (*Emily turns her attention back to the stage.*) Good morning Anthea.

Anthea. I'm fine thank you.

Emily. A little preoccupied today?

Anthea. That's nice. I want you to know though that I really hate Saturday mornings.

Emily. You do?

Anthea. Because I just do. I mean I know they're supposed to be nice and relaxing but I just hate them.

Emily. I've always enjoyed Saturday mornings.

Anthea. I don't know. Because I never feel like I can get myself and my stuff put together when I'm not rushed. If I'm rushed I never forget a thing. If I'm relaxed I forget my head. Now why do you think that is?

Emily. I have no idea.

Anthea. Every Saturday it's like this. I know I've forgotten something but I can't think what.

Emily. I don't see how you could forget anything with all that.

Anthea. I know. Isn't it insane? I'm crazy I know. They should lock me away in a tiny room. But I finally figured out why I have to carry all this — because last night I suddenly remembered that when I was a baby my mother would always forget my diapers whenever we went anywhere. I think I'm still afraid of having to sit in wet diapers. What do you think?

Emily. Is it likely to happen? I mean what happened last

2

night?

Anthea. Nothing. Why? What makes you think something happened?

Emily. Well you said last night you figured it out. So I thought that maybe something happened that made you figure it out.

Anthea. No of course not. Nothing happened. I mean, why does everyone think that something has to happen. I mean not you, you know, but like everybody else always thinks something has to happen. I just don't understand. Is anyone here yet?

Emily. Just you and me.

Anthea. Oh good. It's so much easier when it's just you and me. (Anthea sees the coffee.) Food. Yay! May I please have one of these muffins?

Emily. You know you can.

Anthea. Emily, you're so good to me. You're going to make me fat though, as fat as Shelly Winters. God that's so awful of me. I mean the poor woman had to gain all that weight for the Poseidon Adventure and I'm making fun of her. I should be shot.

Emily. Don't say that.

Anthea. I should, I know it. Go ahead Emily, admit it. You really want to shoot me with a rifle don't you?

Emily. Why are you saying that?

Anthea. (pulls out a doll) Look what I found. (She immediately puts it back before Emily can see it.)

Emily. I didn't get to see it. What is it?

Anthea. I'm not telling you. It's a present for Rachel.

Emily. Tell me.

Anthea. No. I want it to be a surprise.

Emily. Anthea.

Anthea. Nope, you can pull my teeth out with plyers if you want, but I'm not telling.

3

(Miriam *enters wearing very dark sunglasses but they don't see her right away. She looks anxious but with a hangover.*)

Miriam. Hey. Ummm. Like. Uh. Excuse me?

(*Anthea and Emily turn around and see her.*)

Anthea. Yes?

Miriam. Is this the space where there's a rehearsal for...

Anthea. Are you the new woman?

Miriam. Yes. I guess so. I'm supposed to be in a play.

Anthea. Oh great! Hi. I'm Anthea and this is Emily.

Miriam. Miriam. Where's Rachel?

Anthea. (cautiously, like a question.) I don't know?

Miriam. Are you asking me if you don't know? Cause your voice went up at the end.

Anthea. Oh no. I don't. Know that is. Where she is? I don't know?

Miriam. (*she doesn't care*) Oh good coffee. I was hoping someone would bring some. Thanks to whoever brought it.

Anthea. Emily.

Miriam. (*mistaking Anthea for Emily*) Yea, thanks Emily.

Anthea. Oh no no you got it backwards. I'm not Emily. I'm Anthea. This is Emily. Emily was the one who brought the coffee which she usually does because she always gets here before everyone because she's such an early riser — at least I think she is — I don't know I never really asked her — but anyway she brought the coffee not me. I was just answering for her when you asked because she's so shy and quiet and she usually doesn't speak up for herself...

Miriam. Jesus Christ Emily calm down, you're gonna have a heart attack before the day's over.

Anthea. Oh that's so funny you did it again. I'm not

Emily, I'm Anthea. This is Emily and she's the one who...

Miriam. Oh God who gives a shit. I mean you both look like nice people to me. I don't care what your names are. I'll figure it out later. [(*She lights a cigarette.*) **Neither of you mind if I smoke right?**

Anthea. No.

Emily. No.]

Miriam. So what's this play about anyway?

Emily. Well...

Anthea. Well...

Emily. It's about... uhhh

Anthea. Yes.

Emily. Peace.

Anthea. Peace. Yes it's about peace. That's a certainty.

Miriam. Peace?

Emily. Peace and uhhh... love and...

Miriam. The pursuit of happiness?

Emily. Well

Anthea. Sure.

Miriam. Are you sure you know what this play's about?

Emily. Yes of course.

Anthea. Why would we do it if we didn't know what it was about?

Miriam. You got me. But like... specifically.

Emily. Well what would you say Anthea?

Anthea. Me? Well it takes place in the twentieth century.

Emily. Yes it does. That's a definite. (*Pause.*) Miriam I hate to say it but I don't know what this play's actually about. It's all words. It doesn't make any sense. It's probably just poetry.

Miriam. What?

Anthea. No Emily. It's not poetry. It's about something.

5

Emily. Do you know what it is?

Anthea. Well no but it's there. I mean I know it is. I mean feed me to the sharks if I'm wrong but it's just that we've had so many cast changes and we've never had the chance to really get into the play and see what it's all about. That's all.

Emily. Well that could be true. We do seem to have a lot of problems getting things going.

Miriam. So wait a second. You're telling me you don't know what it's about.

Emily. (Emily and Anthea look at each other first.) I take it you don't have a script yet?

Miriam. No. Rachel only called me a couple days ago after her last friend quit. I said, "Thanks for thinking of me last bitch."

Anthea. Oooooh. I don't like that word.

Miriam. (*Quite hostilely*) And? (*Anthea backs away quickly.*)

Emily. Here Miriam. Just listen. (*Emily opens her script.*) "The Opening. Life is only a metaphor for peace and love. We speak peace. We speak love. We live life speaking peace and love. We must climb the tree of honesty and feed like ravenous horses on the honey of truth, taking to the streets the jewels we have mined from our great mother Gaia. This universal truth should be expressed in the opening through song and dance, kissing and hugging, sharing our mood with the audience."

Miriam. Are you kidding me? Are you trying to ram some joke up my ass?

Emily. I promise I would never try to ram a joke up... that.

Miriam. That's supposed to be a play?

Emily. It's only the opening. It's an interpretive text.

6

Miriam. Oh my God, I knew this was gonna be a bad
day. I mean like I get up and my bird's fucking died
on me, you know?

Anthea. Oh how sad.

Miriam. I know. I only had it a week. My mother
always told me I shouldn't be allowed to have pets.

Anthea. (*Looks as though she is going to cry.*) That's so
sad. (*She goes into a dream state.*)

Miriam. So has anybody told her?

Emily. Told who what?

Miriam. Told Rachel that she'd better keep her day job.

Emily. Well that's it. See.

Miriam. No. What's it?

Emily. This play was written by a friend of hers — her
roommate for what, five years Anthea?

Anthea. (*Waking.*) What? Oh. Five years? I'll be thirty
two.

Emily. Her roommate that she had for a long time.

Miriam. I don't remember any roommate. I mean I only
talked to her like once a year so I guess how would I
know.

Anthea. You're not friends?

Miriam. Depends whether it's a full moon.

Emily. What do you mean?

Miriam. It's a long story.

Emily. No one's here yet.

Miriam. Oh I get it. You're one of those people that
have to know everything. Rachel was my best friend
when we were young. I mean you know, like from
seven on up — all through that time when you've
got those dorky looking haircuts and you smoke
cause you think you're so God damned grown up.

Emily. You're not friends now?

Miriam. Sometimes. Lately we haven't been. It just

depends.

Emily. On what?

Miriam. On whether or not we're in the mood to like each other. We keep getting in these fights.

Anthea. I hate fights.

Emily. Why do you fight?

Miriam. You want a list. You know Rachel's like. She's headstrong, determined and she doesn't listen, and I'm just the opposite. Quiet and polite. (*Miriam smiles to indicate she knows she's not.*)

Emily. Is this going to be a making up?

Miriam. Oh puke no. I'm just doing this to work. I'm not here to make up with her. I'm just here to be in a play. Do my job and go home. Although from what you've read this doesn't sound like a play.

Emily. Well like I said her roommate wrote this and she unfortunately never had the chance to see it produced.

Miriam. Of course not if it sucks.

Emily. She passed away.

Miriam. Who?

Emily. Rachel's roommate.

Miriam. Really?

Emily. I think she died of leukemia.

Miriam. Her lover died of leukemia?

Emily. I don't know. I don't know if they were lovers.

Miriam. When did she die?

Emily. I don't know that either.

Miriam. What about her name?

Emily. I don't know.

Miriam. So like, wait a minute here Anthea.

Anthea. No no I'm Anthea. You're talking to Emily. You know you can remember our names if you remember I'm the taller one and my name starts with an A. And Emily's...

Miriam. Shut up a minute. (*Anthea makes a wounded face and starts digging nervously through her bags.*) So what you're telling me is that we're all in a bad play that nobody understands written by some woman whose name we don't know who died form something that we don't what it is or when it happened and nobody has the nerve to ask a question about it cause Rachel might cry if we do?

Emily. I don't know if I would put it like that.

Anthea. Would either of you like some Lorna Doones?

Miriam. (*taking one*) Thanks. So anyway that's basically it right?

Emily. It's a tribute.

Miriam. To a dead person that none of us knew.

Emily. Well it is that "dead person's" play.

Miriam. So what? Why don't we just go on the Circle Line boat and throw roses in the water or something?

Emily. Well.

Anthea. I'm so sorry about your bird.

Miriam. What bird?

Anthea. Your bird that died.

Miriam. It didn't die, I killed it. (*Pause.*) I'm kidding. God lighten up you two. You think I'd kill my own bird. Don't answer that. (*She smiles at them sincerely.*)

Joanne. (*screaming from offstage*) I said GO AWAY! Leave me alone. Just go home and quit following me! (*Joanne enters. Of the five women in this group, she is the most energetic and artificial. Much of what she does is for dramatic effect, as if she's always on stage. She walks across and throws her stuff down in a feigned fit.*) Oh my God I hate being

9

married. Hi everybody. Oh I don't know you.

Miriam. Of course you don't.

Joanne. You're the new woman?

Miriam. Yes. Who are you?

Joanne. Well I'm Joanne. Didn't Rachel tell you?

Miriam. Tell me what?

Joanne. Who I am.

Miriam. Why would she? Are you famous?

Joanne. No. Not yet anyway. I just thought she would have told you.

Miriam. Because you're going to be famous.

Joanne. Well...

Emily. (*Peacemaking*) Joanne this is our new member Miriam. Miriam this is Joanne.

Miriam. Glad to know you.

Joanne. (*saying it exactly the same way*) Glad to know you. Oh isn't that stupid. I said exactly the same thing. Has that ever happened to anybody else or is it just me?

Miriam. It's just you.

Joanne. Hah! Good one. No really you know — like when somebody you see on the street says, "Hi how are you," and you say, "Hi how are you," exactly the same way. It's so embarrassing I can't even tell you. It's like that myth, you know, of the simultaneous orgasm. It's not at all pleasant like everybody thinks. I mean when I have an orgasm I want everybody who's in the room to watch and help me have it. I mean I know that's selfish but I've always said I'm a selfish person and I don't care, and I hope I've shocked everyone here.

Miriam. (*not shocked, to Anthea*) Hey Andrea, you got any more of them Peek Freens?

Anthea. Lorna Doones. It's Anthe...

Emily. What was all that screaming about Joanne?

Joanne. What screaming?

Emily. Go away go away get the hell out of here?

Joanne. Oh that. That was just that damn Eddie.

Miriam. Who's Eddie?

Joanne. He's my husband.

Miriam. Oh you're married. Good for you. How long?

Joanne. Six miserable months.

Miriam. Why miserable?

Joanne. Oh who knows. I don't know. Does anybody know? I don't know. God knows. I don't.

Miriam. Huh?

Emily. Why were you screaming at him?

Joanne. Because he was there. He was bothering me like always. Following me all over the place. It's like I get up in the morning, I eat breakfast and get dressed, and then I get ready to leave and he says, "Oh wait, I'll walk you." Can you believe that? (*She stands indignantly, her hand on her hip.*)

Miriam. Sounds like a real bummer.

Joanne. It is. Have you ever been married Miriam?

Miriam. Yea once when I was in high school. Had a baby and everything.

Anthea. Ohhhh... you had a little baby?

Miriam. No Andrea, I had a teenager. I was like, "Oh my God, what the fuck just came out of me?"

Emily. Boy or girl?

Miriam. Girl.

Emily. Where is she?

Miriam. I don't know. State took her. (*Pause.*)

Emily. They took your baby?

Miriam. Well my mother didn't want it. (*Pause.*)

Anthea. Sometimes you say really sad things.

Miriam. Oh please don't pity me, I get enough of that

from... I say it's all how you look at it. The way I look at it is that kid would be eleven years old and getting on my nerves by asking me day and night when she's gonna grow some tits. At least if she's like me she would. I'm glad they took her — put her in some home that's strong enough to raise her right and be patient with her. I've always said you gotta be real about things — and the real thing is that I just don't have the patience to raisea kid. She's better off not knowing where she's from. (*Pause.*) So what are you all looking at?

Joanne. Anyway girls, Eddie says to me this morning, "I'll walk you to rehearsal," and I said, "Would you quit following me and go do something on your own and enjoy yourself for once," and he says, get this, "I enjoy myself whenever I do something for you." Can you believe that? What an ass-wipe.

Emily. What's wrong with having someone do something for you?

Joanne. He's just doing it to make me feel guilty about hating him. (*Pause.*) So where's our director?

Anthea. She's not here.

Joanne. Well dammit, where the hey is she?

Anthea. I don't know.

Joanne. I mean we should get through at least one read through before someone quits again don't you think? OH GOD WHY IS HE DOING THIS TO ME?

Miriam. Who?

Joanne. That damn Eddie. Oh well I don't really care I suppose. Does anybody have a gun? (*She laughs.*) Whoops, what a slip. I mean a file?

Anthea. I do.

Emily. Have some coffee Joanne.

Joanne. Oh no no. Not for me. Or "pas pour moi" as

they say in Canada. Oh God, Canada. I stay away from caffeine. I mean I'm too wound up as it is don't you think? Sometimes I can't stop talking and I'll be sitting there talking about something while in my mind, you know, up here (*she points at her head*) I'll be having a completely different conversation and then I start to have a third conversation somewhere else where I'm thinking, "Why am I having all these different conversations? And then it all stops and I'm back in the middle of the first conversation and I don't even know what I'm talking about or where I left off. So I try to stay away from caffeine."

(*While Joanne is explaining how her mind works, she takes the file from Anthea and sets it down without using it. Anthea then takes it back and returns it to her bag. Rachel enters carrying a large bag.*)

Rachel. Good morning women.

Joanne. Well finally Rachel. I mean, "My God," as they say in the Hamptons. Oh God, the Hamptons.

Rachel. It's two minutes before ten. I'm not late.

Joanne. Well I've been sitting here for at least half an hour talking about all my problems which I'm sure just bored everyone to tears. (*Joanne laughs very loudly. No one else does.*) You guys that was a joke.

Miriam. Really?

Joanne. I can't believe you all didn't laugh. Does that mean it's true, that I really do bore you to tears?

Emily. Joanne...

Joanne. Do I Emily? Is that it? Do I bore you to tears? I mean I don't know. Do you know. Does anybody know? I don't know. I'm so upset.

Emily. Joanne, it's not that you're boring us. It's just that it was such a terrible joke we didn't even realize that it was one.

Joanne. You're not bored?

Emily. I'm not.

Joanne. Thank you Emily. You're so nice to me. (*She grabs Emily and bear hugs her.*)

Emily. (*Pulling away*) I know.

Rachel. (*Rachel looks up from where she's been staring blankly at a spot on the wall.*) Oh excuse me women, I was lost in an intriguing thought. Was anybody asking for me?

Emily. How was your Friday night Rachel? (*Joanne starts stretching on the floor.*)

Rachel. It was rather nice. I got a lot of work done. Thank you very much for asking. (*Suddenly sees Miriam and realizes she's "new" to the group. This is their first acknowledgment of each other.*) Oh! Miriam. You're here. I completely forget you were coming. Everyone gather round. I'm sorry and I apologize. Have you all met already?

Miriam. No Rachel we haven't. We just sat around, picked each other's noses and compared boogers.

Joanne. (*Laughs loudly. To Emily and Anthea*) I love people like her.

Rachel. Well Miriam, I can see you haven't held back for formalities as usual.

Miriam. What the fuck for?

Rachel. There might be some people who get offended by your casual brand of gutter talk.

Joanne. Not I.

Rachel. Oh fuck off Rachel, I like everyone here and they can like me the way I am or fuck them I say.

Rachel. Alright fine. Everybody this is Miriam and, as you can all tell, her favorite expression is the f word. She'll use that word at least once a minute, just to warn you. She's here to play Jeannie Marie and is, as you all know, the sixth replacement we've called in during the last six weeks. Let us all pray to whatever Gods may be that Miriam is that last replacement this play will ever need. (*Joanne grabs her script and searches through it.*)

Joanne. Heeyyyy — I thought I was Jeannie Marie.

Emily. You're Beth.

Joanne. I thought you were Beth.

Emily. No I'm Cynthia.

Joanne. Well who am I?

Emily. You're Beth.

Joanne. I'm Beth? But I thought I was Jeannie Marie.

Rachel. Emily is Cynthia. You are Beth. Miriam is Jeannie Marie and Anthea is Zandilla. I'm the director and now that we all know who we are, let's get started so we won't be here 'til the middle of the night like last week going over all our personal problems.

Joanne. But Rachel I've memorized the wrong lines. I memorized all the lines for Jeannie Marie.

Miriam. Jeannie Marie, Andrew, Zandulli, Dickless, who cares? I'll be whoever nobody else is.

Joanne. But...

Rachel. Oh Please! We're supposed to be off book already. Alright Emily is still Cynthia. That much we know. Are you off book Emily? Did you memorize the right lines?

Emily. All three of them. All twenty three words.

Rachel. Good. Anthea is Zandilla. Did you memorize the right lines?

Anthea. Well...

Rachel. Oh help...

Anthea. Well I'm trying but there are so many and those

15

speeches are so long. I don't know all of them and you can dig out my eyes with a fork if you want but I'll learn, I promise, I really will learn all the lines...

Rachel. Yes yes yes but is it the right part?

Anthea. Yes.

Rachel. Fine. Miriam. Here's your script. You're...
(*Rachel looks at Emily for an answer.*)

Beth. (*Emily solves a problem without anyone knowing, by re-assigning Miriam to the Beth part.*) Beth.

Rachel. Beth. And Joanne you are...

Emily. Jeannie Marie.

Rachel. Jeannie Marie.

Joanne. (*She clenches her fists, victorious.*) Yes! Jeannie Marie! Thank you mommy.

Rachel. Don't get disgusting on me Joanne. I woke up with a splitting headache.

Miriam. Dreading the day?

Rachel. I'll ignore the snotty comment Miriam, as usual. Everybody in their places please.

Joanne. Rachel.

Rachel. Joanne.

Joanne. Aren't we going to warm up?

[Miriam. (Lighting a cigarette, to Anthea) You got an ashtray in one of them bags Mary Poppins? (Anthea pulls one out and hands it to her.)]

Rachel. Normally, Joanne, we would. But seeing as how it's been six weeks and we still haven't read ten pages of the work with the same cast and I can hardly remember who the cast even is, no not today. I thought about this long and hard last night. We won't dawdle with warm ups and jazzersize and whatever. We'll just get the fundamental blocking done in addition to what we have. And I've got all the music written down so we'll have that fixed too.

You see once we get an idea of what we're trying to deal with then... you know.

Emily. You know what?

Rachel. Nobody will quit once we have an idea of what this play means. So everybody up and on your feet. Stand in the line please. (*They all move to the "acting area."*)

Miriam. What are we supposed to do?

Anthea. This is the opening. This is where we dance.

Miriam. Dance?

Anthea. Like the script says. We read it earlier. "We speak peace. We speak love. We live life speaking peace and love. This universal truth should be expressed through song and dance, kissing and hugging, sharing..."

Rachel. Oh no! Nooooo.

Joanne. What happened?

Rachel. I forgot to charge this stupid thing. Does anybody have a charger I can borrow? (*Rachel looks at Anthea.*)

Anthea. Probably. (*She gets it.*)

Rachel. Thank whatever Gods may be for Anthea's bottomless bag.

Miriam. Unbelievable.

Joanne. Oh believe it. Anthea is so funny, she's like a portable hardware store.

Miriam. Why?

Joanne. Who knows. Well I'm going to have some coffee "while we're waiting" as they say in the office. Oh God those secretaries.

Miriam. You work in an office?

Joanne. Oh yes.

Miriam. You like doing that?

Joanne. I don't know. Who knows. I just work there to

get away from damn Eddie anyway. He keeps saying, "I'll support you. I'll give you money to work on your acting full time." It's like what else does he want to do to make me hate him?

Miriam. Right. Makes sense. (*taking Emily aside*) So Bernadette, you look like the sensible one, let me ask you something.

Emily. (*After a slight pause*) Yes.

Miriam. Why is it that everyone keeps quitting this play? Is the whole thing like that opening?

Emily. No. Sometimes it's quite different, but there have been a lot of disagreements.

Miriam. About what?

Emily. A number of different things.

Miriam. Oh c'mon you wimp. Tell me.

Emily. Just different things. Really it's too complicated to go into right now.

Rachel. (*Announcing it like it's a significant achievement.*) The unit is charging ladies! Places. (*They all take their places while Rachel looks for the right cassette.*) Oh dear, we have another slight problem.

Joanne. What now mommy?

Rachel. Joanne stop with the mommy thing, please. I don't remember what I'm using for the opening music. It'll just take a minute to find it.

Joanne. I thought you had the order all written down.

Rachel. I do. I have the order. I just don't know where I put the music.

Joanne. Don't you label the folders?

Rachel. Of course I label them... just not the ones I made this week.

Joanne. Why not?

Rachel. I was busy. I work too you know. (*She tries a*

piece. It's the theme music from (Johnny Carson's)
The Tonight Show.)

Anthea. That's the Johnny Carson song.

Miriam. So what you have all the talk show theme
songs on tape too?

Rachel. Yes.

Joanne. Yes?

Rachel. Yes. Johnny Carson, David Letterman, Merv
Griffin, Phil Donahue and Sally Jessy Raphael.
Sixty Minutes too but they don't have music, just
that stop watch ticking away. It's not as interesting.
I'd love to know if Dick Cavett had a theme song.
(*Rachel finds some other music. This one is
someone playing a Chopin Nocturne.*)

Emily. That's very pretty. Who's that?

Rachel. That's my baby brother. He's not very good.

Emily. He sounds terrific to me.

Anthea. I love classical music. It's so peaceful.

Miriam. It bores the shit out of me.

Joanne. I have a feeling that everything bores the shit
out of you. But I like that in a person.

Rachel. (*She finds the correct music.*) Oh here it is. And
look I put it in the folder for opening music. What a
nice surprise. Alright everyone back to the line
please. Joanne coffee down please.

Joanne. Yes mommy.

Rachel. Joanne! No more mommy. Ever.

Joanne. Oh alright. Alright already.

Anthea. (*to Joanne*) I thought you didn't drink coffee.

Joanne. Oh that's not mine.

Rachel. I have such a headache.

Anthea. Would you like some Tylenol?

Miriam. (*laughs*) Go ahead. She bought it in Chicago.

Rachel. That's not funny Miriam. People died from that

19

Tylenol poisoning you know. Alright everyone listen. For the opening we're going to dance — very casual. Very relaxed. And happy.

Miriam. Dance to what?

Rachel. To her favorite song.

Miriam. Whose favorite song? Your dead friend's?

Rachel. Yes. My friend who died.

Miriam. Well what kind of dance are we supposed to do?

Rachel. It's not specified. Just whatever inspires you.

Miriam. How about the "let's all lay down and die" tango?

Rachel. Very funny. Alright ready? (*Rachel turns on the tape and "We Are Family," plays. Anthea, Emily and Joanne do some interpretive dance for a few beats — Joanne as extravagantly as possible. Miriam stands to the side and stares at them as if they're all crazy.*)

Miriam. Hold it please.

Rachel. (*turning off the music*) What's the problem?

Miriam. What are we doing?

Rachel. You're dancing.

Miriam. No kidding. Why are we dancing?

Rachel. For the mood.

Miriam. What mood?

Rachel. The mood of the play.

Miriam. If we're dancing we should be dancing for a reason.

Rachel. The mood is the reason.

Miriam. Rachel what are you? Stupid? The mood will come out by how the actors interact, as characters and actors. There won't be a mood just cause you say hey everyone this is the mood and start with some disco.

Rachel. I think I'll let the audience decide that for themselves Miriam. Thank you for your opinion.

Miriam. Fine. But I'll tell you right now they'll just say what is this crap and leave. What dancing have to do with the play?

Rachel. Have you read the play?

Miriam. No.

Rachel. Have you even looked at the title?

Miriam. (*Looking at the title*) Peace and Love Unfolded. What? (*Joanne tip toes between Miriam and Rachel as if she can't be seen.*)

Rachel. Joanne, *what* are you doing?

Joanne. Oh I'm just getting that last cup of coffee? Does anyone mind?

Anthea. No.

Emily. No.

Miriam. Let me have half. (*This annoys Joanne but she continues to tip toe, pours half the coffee into another cup.*)

Rachel. Miriam. This play is full of different things. It's got song and dance and poetry and proverbs and aphorisms. Sometimes we might not understand it on a first reading but later, after a second and third reading, it will make more sense. It's her ode to the power of life. This mood expression, this song and dance at the beginning of the play, is the best indicator of the mood that we could think of.

Miriam. Well it's not very good.

Rachel. Miriam! Do you *have* to be mean?

Miriam. I'm sorry. I don't care what the theme of the play is. I know what people find funny.

Rachel. Oh right. I'd forgotten how many times people laughed at you in high school.

Joanne. (*Miriam and Rachel stand and fume silently.*

Joanne tip toes between them and leaves Miriam's coffee at Miriam's feet. Joanne returns to her spot and then speaks.) Oh you two went to high school together?

Rachel. Yes. (*Miriam picks up her coffee and sits down, [lights a cigarette], puts on some sunglasses and starts reading an Atlantic Monthly she pulls from her bag.*)

Joanne. Tell me you were in the pep club. (*Neither bother to answer.*)

Emily. Rachel, why don't we just skip the opening today and start with the dialogue? Maybe we can figure out what to do about the opening later.

Rachel. (*nearly to herself*) I knew this was going to happen. Is that fine with everyone?

Anthea. Yes.

Joanne. Yes mommy.

Rachel. Miriam?

Miriam. What?

Rachel. Is that okay with you?

Miriam. Is what okay with me?

Rachel. We're gong to skip the opening for now and start with the dialogue.

Miriam. Sure.

Rachel. Alright you three know where ou sit. Miriam you should stand over there near the wall.

Miriam. (*removes her sunglasses.*) Here?

Rachel. Yes.

(*Anthea, Joanne and Miriam are standing in a line. Emily stands directly behind Joanne. Each character moves forward a step to say their line, then retreats. Emily's character mirrors Joanne's every move and gesture, but says nothing.*)

Zandilla. (Anthea.) PEEEAAACCCEEEE!!!!
Beth. (Miriam.) How do you spell peace?
Jeannie-Marie. (Joanne with Emily mirroring)
   P.I.E.C.E.
Zandilla. P.E.A.C.E.

Zandilla. LOOOOOVE!
Beth. How do you spell love?
Jeannie-Marie. L.U.V.
Zandilla. L.O.V.E.
Beth. It says here in the dictionary: Love. Noun.
   One. Strong affection. Two. Warm
   attachment. Three. Attraction based on
   sexual desire. Four. A beloved person. Five.
   A score of zero in tennis.
Beth and Jeannie-Marie. (*Together, but ominously.*)
   A score of zero in tennis.

Joanne. (*looking at Miriam.*) No no. That's my line.
Miriam. It's yellowed out in my script.
Rachel. Oh no. Emily help me please, who is supposed
   to say that line?
Emily. Well it's Jeannie-Marie's line and I think we
   decided that it was Joanne's part.
Miriam. So the hell am I?
Emily. You're Beth.
Rachel. Okay let's start with Jeannie-Marie's line. And
   what the hey. If you want to do a little more of your
   own blocking go ahead but Joanne, just remember
   that you have a human mirror that has to follow
   your every move.

23

Jeannie-Marie. (*Joanne takes a moment to prepare. Makes a "gift package" wave which Cynthia attempts to mirror.*) A score of zero in tennis.

Beth. Isn't that just the way? You think you're doing okay and then suddenly, wham! Somebody kicks you right in the ass.

Zandilla. It wasn't me.

Jeannie-Marie. It wasn't her.

Zandilla. I only crave peace.

Jeannie-Marie. And don't forget love.

Zandilla. How could I darling?

Beth. (*Miriam reads slowly and incomprehensively*) I didn't say nothin' of the kind.

Jeannie-Marie. Then what did you say?

Beth. I don't remember.

Zandilla. You said you were reading the dictionary. I didn't believe you. Hee hee.

Beth. When did I say that?

Zandilla. Back in the days when I spoke of peace.

Jeannie-Marie. And don't forget love.

Zandilla. How could I darling?

Beth. This doesn't make any sense at all.

Rachel. Just keep going Miriam pleeeeease!

Miriam. I am going Rachel. That's my line. It says right here, "This doesn't make any sense at all."

Rachel. (checking) Oh. Sorry. Please continue.

Beth. This *really* doesn't make any sense at all.

Zandilla. Who, these days, does?

Beth. Somebody I used to know.

Zandilla. Tell me. Quickly. Before I stop
   dreaming.
Beth. This is real life.

Joanne. You know this really doesn't make sense.
   (*pause.*) Rachel?
Rachel. (checks her script to see if it's a line.) Joanne
   darn it. You broke character.
Joanne. But Rachel I don't have a character. Honestly,
   I've been here for four weeks and I still don't know
   how to do this.
Rachel. You're doing fine. I told you we would read
   through it until the script pulls itself together. I
   understand it but that's because I understood her.
   When you come to understand her, then it will make
   sense.
Joanne. Listen since we've stopped I'm going next door
   for coffee. Anybody want anything?
Miriam. Barbecue chips. Big bag.
Joanne. I don't usually drink coffee but today I need it
   because of that damn Eddie. He's probably waiting
   outside. God what a pest. Hey you all never met
   Eddie have you? You want to meet him?
Rachel. Joanne we're in the middle of a rehearsal.
Joanne. Since we've stopped anyway. C'mon Emily,
   Anthea. We'll go say hi and then I'll yell at him and
   we'll leave. (*Joanne grabs Emily and Anthea by the
   hands and starts dragging them.*) We'll let Rachel
   and Miriam to talk about old times and
   cheerleading. Ahem. (*She drags both of them off,
   both of them looking back helplessly.*)
Emily. We'll try to hurry.
   (*Rachel is upset and looks briefly at Miriam on the
   other side of the room who has put on her*

sunglasses again. Rachel leans against the wall and stares into space as Miriam stares at her.)

Miriam. Lost in an intriguing thought?

Rachel. What?

Miriam. Skip it. *(Miriam looks around the room taking it all in.)* What a dump.

Rachel. *(after a long difficult pause.)* Are those new sunglasses?

Miriam. *(pulling them off.)* These? Yes. I'm a nut when it comes to sunglasses. Can't pass a stand without buying a pair.

Rachel. Still like high school.

Miriam. Here. *(She pulls out an odd looking pair from her bag.)* Try these on.

Rachel. Oh no.

Miriam. Come on.

Rachel. I'll look ridiculous.

Miriam. You always look ridiculous. Try them on.

Rachel. If you insist. *(She puts them on.)* Happy now?

Miriam. They look good. You should keep them on. You'll intimidate people if you keep them on.

Rachel. Why would I want to intimidate people?

Miriam. For the fun of it.

Rachel. That's not what I call fun.

Miriam. Whatever.

Rachel. *(doesn't remove her sunglasses.)* Do you still hate me?

Miriam. I never hated you. I was mad at you. That's a different thing.

Rachel. Yes but I don't see why you get so mad at me just for wanting to...

Miriam. That's exactly why I get mad at you. I mean, I talk to you barely twice a year and you always want to bring up all that shit. I didn't even know you had

26

a, you know, (*she makes air quotes*) roommate, until today. But you can't resist getting into all that stuff about my past and everything. I was scared to come here but I thought maybe. Give it a shot. Maybe she'll understand that I don't need to know about it.

Rachel. Know about what?

Miriam. About my mother.

Rachel. But if you dealt with it...

Miriam. I have dealt with it.

Rachel. By repressing it? (*Pause*) You have to tell somebody some day.

Miriam. Why? So they can feel sorry for me? Fuck that. (*Pause.*) How did she die? Your roommate?

Rachel. She died of leukemia. Why?

Miriam. Just wanted to know. I don't mean anything. She wrote the play we're in so I wanted to know.

Rachel. Well I'm glad you came today. I've had six people quit on me so far. I'm not sure if I can hold it together much longer.

Miriam. I feel like that every morning. (*They pause but don't look at each other. Rachel removes her sunglasses. Miriam leaves hers on.*) I wonder where that noisy one is with my chips. (*Emily and Anthea run in as Joanne follows, screaming at someone offstage.*)

Joanne. I said go away!

Anthea. We're back.

Joanne. (*throws the small bag of chips at Miriam*) Hi everyone. Here's your chips.

Miriam. And you call this a big bag?

Joanne. I'm sorry, it's just that pest.

Miriam. What'd he do this time? Buy you a new car? (*Everyone laughs.*)

Joanne. No. He was just standing across the street playing his guitar.

Anthea. He's so sweet.

Miriam. He plays the guitar?

Joanne. He thinks so. He plays in Washington Square Park on the weekends. Nobody listens. In fact people tell him to go away. I've seen it happen. Anyway he was over there in front of that ugly building strumming out his favorite song, which is *Moon River*. Oh God why do I love this man? He drives me crazy.

Rachel. Oh gasp. *Moon River*. That gives me an interesting idea. (*She starts writing something in her directing notebook.*)

Miriam. So lemme ask you something Joanne.

Rachel. Excuse me Rachel, please don't start another conversation.

Miriam. It'll just take a second – chill out. What do you do? Or maybe I should ask what are you calm enough to do?

Joanne. I already told you. I work in an office.

Miriam. And do you like that kind of work?

Joanne. Not really, but I work for thee most gorgeous accountant in Manhattan. Every time he comes in the office I get all hot and bothered. Oh my God. Did you hear what I just said? When he comes in the office. I made it sound like he's jerking off behind his desk all the time which I wish he was. Oh God I can't believe how in love with this man I am. As soon as I get a divorce I'm going to start stalking him.

Emily. You're getting a divorce?

Joanne. No. Just wishful thinking. A girl can dream.

Emily. Well that's good. He seems like a very nice man.

Joanne. He can be nice if he takes care of himself, but most of the time he drives me crazy following me around everywhere. He thinks I'm cheating on him which for all my talk I would never do. We'll divorce first, and then I'll cheat on him.

Rachel. (*clearing her throat*) Can we *please* rehearse women?

Joanne. So serious all the time.

Rachel. Well what do you expect Joanne? We have yet to get through a single rehearsal. Last week it was you and Suzanne and Bernice fighting 'til they both quit and before that it was Shelly who quit because she felt you were rubbing it in her face that you were married and she wasn't. And before that it was Janis who quit because she couldn't wear stage make-up — an actor who can't wear stage make up. I ask you. And then before that it was Monique who didn't have any lines and couldn't justify — her words, not mine — "the expenditure of her precious time."

Emily. Rachel, don't worry. The play will be done one way or another. We'll get it done. You just have to have faith and believe that you can solve any problems that occur. It's amateur theatre for gosh sakes.

Rachel. (*grabbing Emily and hugging her*) Thank you Emily. You're so nice to me. You're not going to quit because you have a small part are you?

Emily. (*muffled, because she is being bear hugged*) No.

Rachel. (*to Anthea*) And you're not going to quit because you have to wear stage make up are you?

Anthea. I don't think so?

Rachel. (*to Miriam*) And you...

Miriam. Don't ask.

Rachel. (*finally letting go of Emily.*) Miriam you've made a commitment.

Miriam. I haven't heard most of the play. How do I know? So far it sounds like junk.

Rachel. It's not junk.

Miriam. I said "So far."

Rachel. None of it's junk.

Miriam. Everybody says some it's garbage and it doesn't sound like a play that needs a plot. So why don't you cut out the bad stuff and leave whatever good stuff is left.

Joanne. Cause we'd only have a ten minute play. (*She laughs loudly at her joke.*)

Rachel. That is not why! It's her play. I want to do it the way she would have done it. She was the theatre person not me. And I have to trust her and I will not cut or rewrite or edit one single word. It's her play not mine. All the people who quit were her friends, not mine. This is for her.

Miriam. But I didn't even know this chick.

Rachel. This "chick" Miriam, happened to be a very good friend of mine and I would appreciate it if you talk about her respectfully please. It's one thing to be sarcastic about the living but to be sarcastic about the dead is not only mean, but cheap.

Miriam. What did I say that was sarcastic?

Rachel. Oh never mind never mind. Just get in the line. Try to do something good and worthwhile and everybody stands in the way and knocks you over like you were a garbage can.

Miriam. If the shoe fits.

Rachel. Shut up and stand in the line.

Miriam. Where's this line supposed to be?

Anthea. Up here? (*Anthea indicates an imaginary line*

that stretches across the stage.)

Miriam. Do you always put it like a question when you say anything?

Rachel. Miriam, just please shut up and grab the end of the rope while I find the music. It's the way she talks. She's extremely pusillanimous.

Miriam. (*laughing*) Pussy what?

Rachel. Pusillanimous. It means shy or reticent or cowardly or something like that.

Anthea. (*visibly nervous about being talked about. Takes some shortbread from her bag.*) Would anyone like some shortbread?

Joanne. I would thank you. (*She takes one and then realizes something.*) Hey. We're missing someone aren't we? Who's going to play The Silent One?

Rachel. Oh my life.

Miriam. What's the silent one?

Emily. Look on the cast of characters page Miriam.

Miriam. (*reading aloud*). "The Silent One. A woman who is always onstage but never speaks or interracts with the other four. She represents the un-consecrated woman: the woman in all women who never emerges, even when alone with other women." Are you saying there's a fifth part?

Rachel. Yes.

Miriam. Well who plays her?

Rachel. I. . .will be playing that part.

Joanne. You?

Rachel. Yes. Me. I know I'm not an actor and I'm not a theatre person, but the part is silent and symbolic so I'm going to do it myself. I won't have to act. Now can we please start the tug of war?

(*Anthea, who is the prop person, gets some soft rope from her bag and hands one end to Miriam*

31

*who takes it without complaint. She tries during
the following back and forth, to give the other
end to Joanne, who keeps brushing her away.*)
Joanne. But how are you going to direct and be in the
play?
Rachel. There's nothing to do. The Silent One just sits
on stage the whole time. That's why Monique quit.
Or have you forgotten.
Joanne. What if you get stage fright?
Rachel. I won't.
Joanne. But what if you do?
Rachel. I won't.
Joanne. But what if you do?
Rachel. Are you just being a child now?
Joanne. I don't know are you just being a child now?
Rachel. Joanne, please stop talking and grab the end of
the rope.
Joanne. I'm not talking.
Anthea. (*To Emily.*) Do you think there's going to be
another fight?
Emily. I hope not. That would make seven fights in
seven weeks.
Anthea. (*Starting a "movie game.*) "Seven brides for
Seven Brothers."
Emily. "The Seven Samurai."
Miriam. (*Thinks she gets it.*) Seven-Eleven.
Emily. No it's supposed to be a movie.
Miriam. Oh umm. Seven. Seven. "Seven Up."
Emily. That's a drink.
Miriam. No it's a movie too. This great documentary.
Joanne. Eddie only drinks coffee.
Rachel. Can't you all ever stop talking?
Anthea. I'm sorry? (*Anthea gets the rope which has
been dropped and hands it to Joanne. She takes the*

32

other end herself.)

Rachel. Anytime you're ready.

Miriam. Where am I supposed to stand?

Rachel. I don't know. Just stand over there.

Miriam. By Katrina? (*She means Emily.*)

Rachel. Yes that's fine. (*She starts the music — a Philip Glass piece.*) Ok please begin.

(*Joanne and Anthea prepare to play tug of war. Anthea suddenly pulls the rope out of Joanne's hands, saying her line [as Zandilla] first.*)

Zandilla. Peace.

Joanne. I wasn't ready.

(*They prepare again and start pulling the rope with each word they say, like two lumberjacks using a two man saw.*)

Zandilla. Peace.

Jeannie Marie. Love.

Zandilla. Peace.

Jeannie Marie. Love.

Zandilla. Peace.

Jeannie Marie. Love.

Zandilla. Peace.

Jeannie Marie. Love.

Beth. (*played by Miriam, who just says her line from where she stands.*) Peace and Love do not fight.

(*They continue to saw, using the rope, and exaggerate the "drama" of their words.*)

Zandilla. Peace.

Jeannie Marie. Love.

Zandilla. Peas.

Jeannie Marie. Carrots.

Zandilla. Spinach.

Jeannie Marie. Squash.

Zandilla. Vegetables.

Jeannie Marie. Food!

Zandilla. Life!

Jeannie Marie. Earth!

Zandilla. (*gasps.*) But who wins?

(*They both drop the rope and but Zandilla drops to the ground and starts to cry.*)

Rachel. Wait! Let me change the music. That was very good ladies. Very exciting.

Miriam. I thought you were supposed to be the Silent One.

Rachel. Sorryyyyy.

Miriam. What's all this shit with the music anyway?

Rachel. Shush. I think this is it. (*She starts playing Debussy's first arabesque.*) Now while the music's playing, you, Beth, see Zandilla crying and you cross over to console her.

Miriam. Why?

Rachel. Because you feel sorry for her.

Miriam. Why?

Rachel. Because she's crying.

Miriam. That ain't my fault.

Emily. (*Making a suggestion*) Your character is a very loving person.

Miriam. You're kidding,

Rachel. Don't make it sound so undesirable Miriam. You should try it sometime.

Miriam. So what am I supposed to do?

Rachel. Walk *slowly* over to Zandilla and hug her.

(*Miriam starts to cross but as she's almost reached Anthea, Anthea uses her fingers to make the sign of a cross and holds it up in front of Miriam's face. Anthea looks at her fingers, horrified, but Miriam laughs loudly. Rachel shuts off the tape.*)

34

Rachel. Anthea!

Anthea. Oh my God I don't know why I did that. I'm so
   sorry. I can't believe I did that. That was so mean.
   You should beat me with a stick or something.

Miriam. Jesus Emily calm down. It was just a joke. I
   know I...

Anthea. Why are you always forgetting my name! I'm
   sorry. I shouldn't have yelled. I'm so sorry. I'll lie
   down on the floor and you can step on my face. I
   never yell like that. It's just that yesterday was so
   embarrassing and all so I guess I'm just testy today.
   I mean if you don't remember my name that's not
   your fault. If you want to punish me go right ahead.

Miriam. Why the hell would I want to punish you?

Joanne. What happened yesterday?

Anthea. What do you mean?

Joanne. You said yesterday was so embarrassing.

Anthea. No I didn't.

Joanne. Yes you did.

Anthea. I don't think so.

Emily. Anthea what happened?

Anthea. Nothing? Please don't make me tell.

Emily. You can tell us. We care about you.

Anthea. (*pointing at Miriam.*) She doesn't.

Miriam. I don't even know you.

Anthea. Oh God! Why am I saying these things?
   What's wrong with me? Somebody should throw
   me out of a building. They really should.

Miriam. Anthea... (*nods or gestures to indicate she used
   the right name.*) I may not seem nice but actually I
   am really nice. I don't hate anyone until I've known
   them for at least two weeks.

Emily. Why don't you just tell us what happened
   yesterday.

Anthea. (*long pause*) I had an audition.

Joanne. That's what you're upset about?

Anthea. It was for a commercial.

Joanne. But that's fantastic.

Emily. I'm jealous.

Anthea. It's not that. It's the type of commercial.

Miriam. What about it?

Anthea. I just don't want anybody to laugh?

Emily. No one will laugh.

Anthea. It was an audition for... an adult... diaper.

Miriam. Adult diapers?

Anthea. For people will bladder control problems.

(*Joanne laughs but Emily looks at her and silences her.*)

Anthea. See.

Emily. It only sounds funny at first. Why are you upset about it?

Anthea. I don't have a bladder control problem.

Joanne. Nobody said you did.

Anthea. You don't understand. I got the job. I got it. I got a commercial.

Joanne. But that's fantastic.

Emily. It's incredible.

Anthea. No it's just... is that what they think I look like? Do I look like someone with a problem like that?

Emily. Anthea, you know as well as I do that that has nothing to do with it. They hired you because you look good on camera or read well.

Miriam. You don't have to do it.

Anthea. I auditioned. I didn't think I was going to get it. I go to hundreds of auditions like all of you and you know how many thousands of people show up for a little part with one or two lines. And everybody says if you want to be a working actress you'll do anything — take anything — anything at all — no matter how good or bad the job is or who you're working with, or if you have to pretend to like some of the people you're working with even if you don't. And I'm embarrassed and I feel stupid for being embarrassed.

Miriam. So just don't do it.

Anthea. But I auditioned.

Miriam. So? You don't have to take everything you're offered. You made a mistake.

Anthea. But how would that look? I'd get a reputation.

Miriam. You don't have to care what anyone thinks.

Rachel. You certainly know a lot about insensitivity.

Miriam. Eat shit and die Rachel. I'm very sensitive. I just don't think anyone should do or say something they don't want to do or say. That's how I live my life and Andrea here's all upset because she can't say no to these people.

Rachel. She's upset because you can't remember that her name is Anthea.

Miriam. (*Looks at Anthea, realizes her mistake.*) She doesn't care. She knows I like her. Except for the habit of phrasing everything like a question.

Anthea. You like me?

Miriam. Of course I like you, I don't know you yet. Anyway if you want I'll come over and help you tell these people to find someone else to piss all over themselves.

Anthea. But you're different. You can say anything you want and it never bothers you. I could never do that. Everything I say bothers me. I could never say how it drives me crazy that Joanne complains about her husband so much.

Joanne. Eddie?

Anthea. I mean, yes. Eddie. He seems so nice and all you did is complain about him. And I could never every say that, at least not to your face.

Joanne. Listen you, just because I'm married doesn't mean I have nothing to complain about. In fact, it probably means that I have more to complain about. (*Pause.*) Anthea?

Anthea. Me?

Joanne. Yes. You just said I complain too much about Eddie.

Anthea. No I said I could never say that. I meant it as an example.

Joanne. But it's what you think isn't it? (*Pause.*) Isn't it?

Anthea. (*After a very long pause.*) I can't say.

Emily. I think what Anthea might mean, Joanne, is that you might not appreciate, in spite of all the problems of marriage, how fortunate you are to have found something that the rest of us never seem to find.

Joanne. Millions... no billions of women find it all the time and billions of women don't like it.

Emily. Well yes you're right.

Joanne. I mean I don't see why I have to shut my mouth. Why can't I complain if I'm not happy.

Anthea. But all you do is complain! Oh my God. I'm sorry. I'm sorry. I shouldn't yell. Just throw cheese on me or something. I'm sorry.

Miriam. Don't apologize Anthea, yell at the bitch. Tell her what you think.

Joanne. I have a lot to complain about.

Anthea. But it never changes does it? It never gets better and it's always about how horrible he is for doing all these nice things. I don't even know if a guy has ever bought me flowers. Women have. Friends I mean. But a guy who buys you flowers just because he wants to. It's just so nice.

Joanne. You don't know anything about it Anthea. In fact I think you're jealous.

Anthea. I'm not jealous, I'm lonely. (*Pause.*) And I really wish I didn't have to talk about this anymore because I always feel like I'm going to start crying.

Joanne. I'm lonely too you know. Eddie is a premature ejaculator and you have no idea how lonely that makes me feel. I mean sometimes he's not even in the room and I hear him go, "oops."

Miriam. Yea what a tragedy. Frankly I'd settle for a Two Pump Chump right about now. It's been a couple of months since I had a good tonsillectomy. What about you Emily?

Emily. Pardon?

Miriam. You seeing anyone?

(*Emily starts to clean.*)

Emily. Oh no.

Joanne. I thought you said you had a boyfriend.

Emily. No I never said anything like that.

Joanne. Did you used to?

Emily. No.

Miriam. Never?

Emily. No. (*Sighs.*) Do we really have to talk about this?

Joanne. You've never had a boyfriend.

Emily. No. Never. I've never had a boyfriend. Isn't that amazing.

Joanne. Can I ask you something personal? (*Emily doesn't respond.*) Are you a virgin?

Emily. No I'm not.

Joanne. I don't understand.

Emily. I guess, Joanne, no guy has ever liked me or thought I was pretty or anything.

Joanne. You're very pretty.

Emily. No I'm not.

Joanne. Yes you are.

Emily. I know that I'm not Joanne. Stop telling me that I am. I learned at a very young age that I wasn't pretty, just like every girls learns at a very young age that pretty, is what she's supposed to be.

Rachel. Okay I have to interrupt here. We are not here to talk about men, or about the ones you don't have. We're here to rehearse and hopefully, one day, within our lifetimes, perform a play my friend wrote. We are here for a cause, not ourselves — and all this talk about not having men really annoys me.

Joanne. Well that's ridiculous, I have a man.

Rachel. I'm not talking about you. I'm saying that you all seem to think that a man is the reason you're alive. You're depressed because you think that without a man you aren't good people, which is completely untrue. You are wonderful, talented and beautiful people and I mean that. And I wish you wouldn't sit here thinking that men are the reason you're put on earth.

Miriam. I don't think that. I don't think any of us do.

Rachel. It's all you've been talking about for the last ten minutes.

Miriam. We've been talking about sex.

Rachel. You've been talking about men.

Miriam. Because we've talking about sex and some of us need men for sex. Get it?

Rachel. (*Turns abruptly, embarrassed.*) Oh it doesn't matter anyway, I'd just like to get through this rehearsal so if you'll all get in your places please.

Joanne. I don't feel like rehearsing anymore.

Rachel. Joanne, in fact, everyone, please. This is not group therapy. I'm sorry if you're not getting enough satisfaction in that area but don't think about what you don't have. You should think about what you do have, which is us and this play. And as Emily whatever you think of this play now, it'll be a good one, if you make it good. It's rhythm. It's rhyme. It's poetry and it's joy, ultimately. And it'll be a good play if you make it good. So please, will everyone just take their places. Please?

Miriam. (*Genuinely.*) Where are the places? This is my first rehearsal remember?

Rachel. Stand next to Joanne please.

(*Rachel starts searching for whatever piece of music she needs, but can't find it. The Tonight Show theme music plays. She turns it off quickly.*) I'm sorry ladies I've been trying to record music all week and I haven't had time to get everything put in the proper order. Everything has the wrong names. I don't under... (*The voice of a woman who is crying or sobbing plays, which Rachel is initially shocked to hear and then fumbles to turn it off.*)

A Woman. And I just have to go to that place. I can't live in this kitchen so much like a roach...

Emily. Who was that?

Rachel. No one. Just a clip from a television movie. (*She gets Joni Mitchell's Unchained Melody to play.*) Why don't you all start because I'm not sure where the right song is. I can get Moon River later and when Joanne mentioned that Eddie was singing it across the street.

Joanne. It's Eddie's favorite song.

Miriam. More irrelevance. (*Joanne sticks her tongue*

out.) Rachel what am I supposed to do here? I mean what's my blocking?

Rachel. Just stand there and keep up. Whoever's first just start reading please and I'll play the music.

(*Anthea prepares with some deep breathing.*)

Zandilla. Do you yearn for peace?

Beth. I yearn for peas and carrots.

Cynthia. Thank you for coming Zandilla.

Zandilla. Do you yearn for peace?

Cynthia. Thank you for coming Zandilla.

Jeannie Marie. I'd love a piece of cheese.

Beth. Or a slice of cheese pizza.

Joanne. A piece of cheese pizza.

(*Emily steps away from her place in the line. She has "left" the play and is now with the audience. She watches the other women.*)

Zandilla. A piece of cheese peace, uh.

Jeannie Marie. Peace uh? I've never heard of Peace uh.

Beth. What's peace got to do with it?

Zandilla. Peace and love is everything.

Beth. Peace is freedom from disturbing thoughts or emotions. Love is a score of zero in tennis.

Zandilla. Jeannie Marie. (*Together*) A score of zero in tennis.

(*Emily speaks to the audience now. The others continue to move as if they're reading, stepping forward from the line whenever it's their turn to speak. Their movements will stop and they will freeze after the three lines they have in the middle of Emily's monologue. Rachel turns off Joni Mitchell and steps back to watch the scene. At some point during Emily's monologue, Moon River begins. It should be timed so that the song ends as the lights go down on the last line of the act.)*

Emily. I had three lines. I had all the time in the world to observe. It seems all my life I've had the time to pull back and watch. It isn't exactly a fun way to live but it helps me see things. That day, the day Miriam joined out troupe, I saw a war brewing. It had something to do with Rachel and Miriam, aggravated by Joanne, and observed with mild frustration by Anthea and me. I think it was happening because we were all pretending. Anthea – (*Anthea steps out for one of her movements or lines*) – pretending to be the same when she had just confronted Joanne about her complaints about Eddie. Rachel — (*Rachel moves to search for something*) — pretending that her friend had died of leukemia when we all knew that she had committed suicide. Miriam — (*Miriam steps out.*) — I wasn't sure about. It seemed that she was pretending something, but in a different way — sort of like the way Joanne — (*Joanne steps out*) — pretending to hate and loathe Eddie when you knew she love him. And me — (*Emily faces the audience*). Well I was just as guilty. While they were reading those horrible lines in a play that always seemed to be on the verge of making sense but never quite getting there:

Zandilla. Peace.

Beth. Piece of liver.

Jeannie Marie. This is of my liver which is given for thee. Take, eat. And remember. It's good with fried onions.

Emily. While they were reading those lines and I had to wait for thirty pages until I had my last line, I drifted. I thought about how Joanne had hurt my

feelings when she asked me about boys... men. How I pretended it didn't matter... because they didn't care anyway, except maybe Anthea. What's the point of getting upset about something if no one else is going to care? All my life nobody's cared. I could have told them that when I was in college and wanted to lose my virginity that I summoned up all my courage and asked this guy who I thought was really nice if he would like to sleep together. And how he said give me five dollars first. And how I gave him the five dollars which he handed back with a laugh, saying it was a joke, thank God, except it didn't feel like a joke. I could have told them how I've felt all my life that I was born for only two incompatible reasons: to be ignored and to be an actress. So I'm an actress that gets three lines in a bad play. Perfect balance of shame and attention. But I didn't tell them anything. I shut my mouth and pretended. I pretended that I didn't feel like puke. Because there was one time I couldn't pretend and had started crying at the dinner table. It was after my mother died. I was eight. It's something I remember whenever I feel this low and get one of my daily headaches. My father had taken me into our living room and asked me why I was crying. I said I didn't know, which was true. And so he said, "Alright Emily, here's what you do. Put your chin up, your shoulders back, make a pretty smile and tell yourself, I will not cry." (*In voice like she might have used at the age of eight.*) "I will not cry daddy. I promise I will not cry anymore." (*And in a voice as her adult self.*) "I will not cry."
(*She doesn't. Emily returns to "The line," and the same position she was before. The lights are facing*

and Moon River is ending. The women finish the
last lines of the scene of the play. It should,
hopefully, sound somewhat beautiful.)
Beth. Peace and love.
Jeannie Marie. Peace and love.
Zandilla. Peace and love is everything.

Fade to black.

End of Act I.

ACT II

(The lights rise very slowly, only coming to full at the end of this scene. This is what they were reading as Emily "drifted" at the end of the last act. Moon River should be playing.)

Beth. How do you spell hate?

Jeannie Marie. R.O.L.A.I.D.S. *(Joanne laughs loudly. [The joke was based on a well known commercial of the time.])*

Rachel. Joanne please.

Jeannie Marie. H.A.I.G.H.T.

Zandilla. H.A.T.E.

Beth. Hate. Noun. One. Intense hostility and aversion. Two. An object of hatred. Verb. One. To find distateful. Two. To express of feel extreme resentment.

Zandilla. To feel extreme resentment.

Jeanne Marie. That's just about the dumbest thing I've ever heard. I hate lima beans but I don't resent them. How could you resent a lima bean?

Beth. I love food. All food.

Jeannie Marie. But do you want to be a lima bean?

Beth. I have to confess, though it makes me feel a wee bit foolish. Yes. I do.

Zandilla. Don't feel sad honey. They understand why you can't be one of them.

Beth. Who does?

Zandilla.The lima beans.

Beth. But they don't understand what we live with.

Jeannie Marie. What's that?

Beth. War.

Zandilla. And hate.

Jeannie Marie. But ain't we got peace and love.

Zandilla. Only in minute rice doses.

Jeannie Marie. Oh what a life. What a ponder.

Beth. Of peace.

Jeannie Marie. Peace.

Zandilla. Peace.

Beth. And love.

Jeannie Marie. Love.

Zandilla. Love.

Beth. Peace and Love.

Jeannie Marie. Peace and love.

Zandilla. Peace and love is everything.

(*Moon River ends. Rachel gives a genuinely appreciative applause.*)

Rachel. Excellent women. So pretty and poetic. Anthea your delivery was especially beautiful. Now at least we can finally get something done.

Miriam. Are you kidding? I've never heard so much crap jammed into a couple of minutes since the last presidential press conference.

Rachel. Now that is really uncalled for Miriam.

Joanne. Well girls I'm going next door for more coffee. Anybody want anything? Coffee cake? I'm buying.

Rachel. Joanne?

Joanne. Yes.

Rachel. We're rehearsing.

Joanne. I know that but I didn't have breakfast and I'm feeling faint. Do you want anything Miriam?

Miriam. Get me some Twinkies. No. Black and White cookie.

Joanne. Em? I'm buying.

Emily. No thank you.

Joanne. How about you Rachel? I'm buying.

Rachel. I want us to rehearse.

Joanne. Anthea?

Anthea. Umm... well if it's not out of your way... would
    you mind getting me a diet soda?
Joanne. Of course.
Anthea. (*Starts digging through her purse.*) Let me give
    you some money. I have my wallet here somewhere.
Joanne. I'm leaving. I'm not letting you give me money.
    God I hope Eddie's there. (*She stops.*) I mean... of
    course what I meant is I hope he's *not* there.
    (*Joanne leaves. Anthea continues to dig through her
    purse.*)
Anthea. I have money. I have money. I have a wallet in
    here somewhere...
Miriam. (*Tapping Anthea on the shoulder.*) Hey.
Anthea. What?
Miriam. She's gone.
Anthea. But she didn't let me give her money.
Miriam. Too bad. Deal with it.
Rachel. (*Gestures to Miriam to come over to her.
    Miriam moves to Rachel. Waits.*)
Miriam. What? Speak.
Rachel. (*Quietly.*) Don't ruin this for me.
Miriam. What are you talking about?
Rachel. You heard me.
Miriam. I hear you all the time. I never know what
    you're talking about.
Rachel. Heard, by the way, and... Just. Don't.
Anthea. (*To Emily*) I can't find my wallet. I forgot it. I
    can't find my wallet. How could I forget it?
Miriam. I'm not going to ruin anything Rachel, as long
    as you stay away from a certain subject.
Rachel. I won't talk about that certain subject as long
    you don't ruin this for me. The play is not crap. It's
    poetic.
Miriam. Oh that's it. You're mad that I called it crap.

You're so sensitive. (*She walks away.*)

Emily. Didn't you need it today? You brought coffee this morning.

Anthea. Yes but I used the money from the inside pocket of my bag not that... oh now I remember. I took my wallet out to take the money out to put in the pocket and then I forgot to put it back in. It's because it's Sunday. I hate Sundays.

Miriam. Not me. I love Sundays. I always feel like somebody's dropped a bomb on me Sunday morning, but that's cause Saturday night was such a blast.

Emily. And you like that?

Miriam. At least I know I had fun.

Rachel. It's funny, but I've never had to get drunk to have fun.

Miriam. What makes you think I was drunk?

Rachel. Well whatever it is you do.

Miriam. You ever been drunk?

Rachel. No.

Miriam. 29 years old and you've never been drunk.

Rachel. No.

Miriam. Then you how do you know it's not fun?

Rachel. All you have to do is look at a drunk person to know they're not having fun. They're not human. They're not themselves. They're not honest. They're not...

Miriam. Oh shut up. How about you Emily? You ever been drunk?

Emily. (*Smiling*) This is a funny question.

Miriam. It's not a funny question, it's just a question.

Emily. Well once. Yes.

Miriam. And was it fun?

Emily. Ummm. Do you want the truth or are you just

trying to prove a point to Rachel?

Miriam. (*Taken by surprise for a second, but impressed.*) Guilty as charged. You're not such a wimp are you? Tell my anyway.

Emily. No. I didn't have fun.

Miriam. Why not? Were you with people you didn't like?

Emily. No. I don't ... didn't have fun because I was by myself. And I got depressed about what I was doing and so I tried to fall asleep but everything spun and it wasn't fun. It wasn't fun at all.

Miriam. Well of course not you were by yourself. If you want to get drunk and stupid you've got to be with other drunk and stupid people, otherwise it doesn't work. So okay. You and me tonight. After we take care of Anthea's diaper problem we'll go get drunk and have some fun. We'll take cabs everywhere. Being drunk in a cab is great: roll down the windows and scream things at all the goofy looking people. "Hey asshole with the umbrella, don't do drugs." That kind of thing.

Emily. Well thank you Miriam but I don't think so.

Miriam. Why not? I'm not doing anything tonight. You busy?

Emily. I'm just not the screaming type.

Miriam. (*Pause*). Okay. Well we'll do it another time then. Whenever you want. I'll give you my number. (*Joanne appears, holding a bag in one hand and something behind her back.*)

Emily. (*To Anthea*) Do you have some aspirin?

Anthea. Tylenol.

Emily. Oh. Well thanks anyway. You know they never found who did that.

Anthea. Really?

Joanne. (*Overlapping*). That damn Eddie was there. He gave me something.

Anthea. He gave you a paper bag?

Joanne. (*Pulling a bouquet of roses from behind her.*) Roses! (*She throw them across the room.*)

Anthea. No! (*Anthea runs to retrieve them, gets a vase she has in her bag and puts them on the table.*)

Joanne. He just won't stop. That damn Eddie.

Emily. Why does it bother you to get roses?

Joanne. How would you like it if somebody told you they loved you forty times a day? Or spent every dime, nickel and cent they had on you? Or did everything but jump off a cliff for you?

Emily. I think it would be nice.

Joanne. For a week it was. But it's six months now. It's terrible.

Anthea. But why?

Joanne. Because he doesn't have a life. He does everything for me and nothing for himself. And I know the reason he does everything for me is because he doesn't respect himself. He thinks he can only be happy if I'm happy. But it gets old. It's not a surprise if he does something nice for me because it's just more of the same. Another day of perfection. It's like having Valentine's day every single day of the year and it's nauseating. So I scream at him to try to make him stop but he just keeps at it. I don't know. Does anybody know? I don't know. (*Pause.*) He's a pet; not a husband. Maybe some women would like that, but I don't. You can keep those roses Anthea; I don't want them.

Rachel. Well now that we've had our break for sob story telling, can we start again?

Joanne. That was a mean thing to say... mummy.

Rachel. I'm sorry. It's just that we've spent so much time talking and so little time working on this play... it's just getting very frustrating. So if you would all please stand in the line, except for Emily who should sit.

Joanne. But Rachel I am not doing all the talking.

Rachel. I know that. I didn't say you were.

Joanne. Yes but I just want you to know.

Rachel. I know. I know. Now please.

Joanne. Because I don't like being blamed for something that's not my fault.

Rachel. I'm not blaming you Joanne. Just please get in the line and stop talking.

Joanne. I just told you I'm not talking.

Rachel. You're absolutely right. You're not talking. But please just get in the line.

Joanne. Just let me fix my coffee.

Rachel. If I didn't know better I'd think you enjoy all this arguing.

Joanne. Why would I enjoy arguing?

Rachel. I don't know. I certainly don't enjoy it.

Miriam. What do you enjoy?

Rachel. I am not going to start another conversation about something that doesn't matter Miriam, so if you would please... oh SHIT.

Emily. What's wrong?

Rachel. I left the paper plates at home. (*After a beat she looks at Anthea.*) Anthea. You're like my personal prop mistress. You don't, by chance, have some paper plates in your bag do you? (*Anthea gives her a look to indicate, "what do you think." Crosses to her bag and pulls some out.*) Thank whatever Gods may be. (*Anthea hands the paper plates to Joanne and Miriam.*)

Miriam. What am I supposed to do with this?

Rachel. Draw a smiley face on the back.

Miriam. What?

Rachel. It's for the Andrews Sisters scene. Does anybody have a marker?

Anthea. Guess. Guess. (*She goes to her bag, takes out some markers and hands them to out.*) I can't stand it sometimes, all this stuff I have to carry. I'm so crazy. God forbid I don't have an battery powered fan when I need one. (*Anthea pulls out a hand fan.*)

Joanne. Oh let me try. (*Joanne takes the fan and cools herself. Rachel looks for a musical piece. Anthea, Miriam and Emily sit on the floor and make their smiley faces on the paper plates. The moment is quiet and calm.*)

Joanne. What do you think is the worst age to be?

Miriam. The worst age to be is the day before you notice your first pubic hair.

(*The others stare at Miriam while she concentrates on making her smiley face.*)

Joanne. Ahem. We don't understand Miriam.

Miriam. Because... one day before it all starts to happen you're just about dead from waiting. The day I found my first pubic hair I was so happy. I plucked that thing out, ran to the drugstore and had it laminated.

Joanne. Oh you did not.

Miriam. No of course not. One day I looked down and it had all started. I had a bunch of pubes. Same with my tit buds. All of a sudden they were there. And man was I happy.

Joanne. But why were you so happy?

Miriam. Because it meant that I was getting closer to

getting out.

Joanne. Out of where?

Miriam. Out of my home.

Joanne. Oh. (*Miriam returns to making her mask. The others, after a moment, continue their tasks. They all seem to want to ask questions of Miriam. Rachel acts cautious, as if she knows something.*) Oh what a nut.

Emily. Who?

Joanne. I was just thinking about that damn Eddie.

Miriam. If they make your life into a movie...

Joanne. What do you mean if?

Miriam. When... they make your life into a movie they're gonna call it "That darned cat."

Anthea. That Girl.

Miriam. The Girl From U.N.C.L.E.

Anthea. The girl from Ipanema...

(*Joanne gasps, jumps up and starts singing the song. Miriam joins in, as does Anthea and Emily. Anthea and Emily don't really know the words.*)

Joanne. ...goes walking, each time she passes each one she passes goes ahhhh. When she walks she's like a samba that swings so cool and sways so gentle, each time she passes each one she passes goes.... (*Joanne waits for everyone to sing.*)

Everyone (*except Rachel.*) Ahhhhh.

Joanne. Ooooh, but I watch her so sadly. How can I tell her, "I love you?" Yes, I would give my heart gladly....

Everyone (*except Rachel. They should sound good enough that you'd actually like to hear them sing the whole song.*) ...but each day, when she walks to the sea. She looks straight ahead, not at me. Tall and Tan and Young and Lovely, the Girl from

Ipanema...

Rachel. Will you all please stop singing and make your faces? (*Joanne makes some sort of face. Everyone else laughs.*) Such schoolchildren. I can't believe it. I really can't. And I can't find the MUSIIIIIC! (*Rachel plays a couple of different tunes, including "There's No Business Like Show Business," and finally finding the correct piece, "Mr. Sandman."*) Okay this is it. Miriam, please stand next to Joanne with the happy face behind your head and just try to follow along for now. There's only a couple of back and forth moves. Nothing like Michael Jackson and the Billie Jean video. (*Rachel laughs because she thinks she's made a joke. When no one else laughs she moves on quickly.*) Okay. Ready. Go.

(*She starts the music. Anthea and Joanne sing along to Mr. Sandman and dance a very simple side step. At the second verse they turn around, holding their masks to the back of their heads.*)

Miriam, who is trying to keep up, turns around later and holds her mask up, but she has not drawn a smiley face but something more like this:

55

Rachel. What the hell is that?

Miriam. It's my mask.

Rachel. It's supposed to be a smiley face.

Miriam. She is smiling.

Rachel. She is not. Next time do it right please.

Miriam. I don't know if there's going to be a next time.

Rachel. What?

Miriam. I told you over the phone —

Rachel. Miriam please...

Miriam. I told you over the phone that I didn't know if I was going to do this or not. It's like Anthea's adult diaper commercial. (*She pretends to be the scales of justice.*) Should she or shouldn't she. On the one hand, it could lead to more commercials, and money, and jobs. On the other hand, people on the street will say that's the lady that shits herself. I told you I was going to see how this went and so far it just looks like I'm going to be shitting myself.

Rachel. You made a commitment.

Miriam. No I didn't, and I said "so far." I'm not saying I've made up my mind. Maybe there's still something good here.

Rachel. You've still made a commitment.

Miriam. No. You made a commitment. Of me. I didn't make one. You spoke for us both.

Rachel. So is that how you run your life? You have to sign everything first and if you haven't signed anything you can just walk away. Walk away from anyone? With no loyalty? Including to a friend. (*The other three should be looking at each other. There should be a distinct feeling that Miriam and Rachel are not talking about "now."*)

Miriam. I've got plenty of loyalty to a friend. (*Miriam finds her magazine and sits.*)

Emily. Rachel, maybe we can rehearse one of the other scenes and skip the mask scene.

Rachel. (*Looking at Miriam.*) This play is very important to me. In fact it's probably the most important thing I've ever done. I don't care if you don't like it. We're not here to do something we like. I don't know why you're making it so hard for me? (*Miriam doesn't respond.*)

Emily. Do you want to try another scene?

Rachel. (*Tired.*) Again and again and again. Yes let's try another scene. Dammit and we were doing so well earlier. Fine will everyone please skip to page 34 and we'll start where Zandilla says, "Peace and love make the honey of truth digestible." (*The four stand in a line and wait. Rachel says nothing.*)

Miriam. Well come on Rachel. What are you gonna do, stand there and make us watch you pick your nose?

Rachel. (*Very excited, thinking she has just saved the production.*) Shut up Miriam. I just thought of something that might make this whole thing work. Would you mind if I play with the casting a bit? It seems that maybe it would be better if Miriam played Zandilla, Joanne played Beth, Anthea played Jeannie Marie and instead of Emily playing Cynthia,

I'll play that part and Cynthia can play The Silent
One. I think really might be better now that I think
on it because the parts might be better suited to your
individual personalities. What do you all think? Can
we try it? Just to see? Miriam.

Miriam. Sure. It's not like it's gonna change the words.

Rachel. Anthea?

Anthea. Okay?

Rachel. Joanne?

Joanne. As long as I get the same amount of exposure.

Rachel. You can take your top off if you need more.

Joanne. Oh my God thank you. (*Unbuttoning.*)
Wouldn't it be nice to just rehearse topless?

Rachel. I didn't mean it.

Joanne. You're no fun.

Rachel. Good Then let's try it and hope it works. I'll
read my part from here and Emily, you sit over there
for now until we figure out where we should have
you positioned during each part of the play. Okay let
me find the music. I'm so excited.
(*Emily moves to her spot, stunned.*)

Miriam. All these music cues are getting on my nerves.
(*The music comes up. It's something from the 60s
like Nancy Sinatra's Boots, with a rhythm that
makes Joanne GoGo dance.*)

Joanne. Oh my God I love this song. (*Joanne dances all
the way over to the door of the rehearsal space,
oblivious to anything.*)

Rachel. What on earth is wrong with that woman?

Miriam. Maybe she's happy.

Rachel. Don't be ridiculous, nobody's happy. She's a
narcissist is what it is. (*She shuts off the music.*)

Joanne. Hey, I was having fun.

Rachel. That's not the right kind of fun. Now please

just stand next to Miriam. (*Prepares the music.*)
Okay anytime you're ready Miriam, start.
Remember you're Zandilla now.
(*Rachel plays the Banarama song Wish You Were Here. Miriam reads Zandilla as if deeply fatigued.*)
Zandilla. Peace Love make and the honey of truth digestible. We eat honey. Do we eat Peace and Love? How do we digest it? Do we digest food or something larger than ourselves. Are our eyes bigger than our stomachs when it comes to love? Are our stomachs bigger than our brains? And brains bigger than peace and peace bigger than feet and feet bigger than foot and foot bigger than fight and fight bigger than war and war bigger than peace?

Miriam. Holy shit.

Beth. Boy am I hungry.

Jeannie Marie. For peace?

Beth. No. For love.

Zandilla. (*Miriam looks at Emily and laughs.*) Do you ever feel like there's someone with us that never speaks.

Cynthia. (*Now played by Rachel.*) I love you all very very very very very very very very much.

Zandilla. What a beautiful thing to say Cynthia.

Jeannie Marie. Anybody got some food?

Zandilla. I have peace.

Jeannie Marie. Did you say peas?

Zandilla. With love.

Jeannie Marie. Did you broth? Peas with broth?

Beth. A score of zero in tennis.

Zandilla. Peace.

Beth. Freedom from disturbing thoughts or emotions.

Zandilla. Do you two believe in peace and love?

Beth. Why of course.

Jeannie Marie. Sure hon. But right now I'd believe a lot more in a pastrami on rye with plenty of mustard and mayo.

Zandilla. Are you willing to digest the honey of truth?

Jeannie Marie. Right now I'll digest any fucking thing you put in front of me.

Rachel. (*Interrupting*) There's no "fucking" in the script Joanne.

Joanne. I was in the moment.

Zandilla. What is peace and love?

Beth. I told you before. Peace. Freedom from disturbing thoughts or emotions. Love. A score of zero in tennis.

Zandilla. Shall we roll on the floor?

Beth. (*Getting to her knees.*) Yes the floor.

Jeannie Marie. The floor?

Zandilla. The floor.

Jeannie Marie. Why do you want to roll on the floor?

Zandilla. Because it's not really there.

Beth. Where?

Zandilla. There.

Jeannie Marie. It's covered with honey.

Beth. The honey of truth?

Jeannie Marie. And we need to roll in it.

(*Jeannie Marie and Beth lie down on the floor to roll. They start singing from where they are lying.*)

Jeannie Marie. Let's all roll for peace.

Beth. Let's all roll for love.

(*They start to roll back and forth. Miriam*

(Zandilla) looks on almost in horror and covers her mouth as she laughs.)

Jeannie Marie. Peace and love.

Beth. Peace and love.

Jeannie Marie and Beth. Let's all roll for peace and love.

Miriam. (*Laughing.*) Please stop it. Stop it! This has got to be the most ridiculous and degrading thing I've ever partially heard in my entire life. I'm sorry folks. I'm not doing this play.

Rachel. (*Shutting off the music.*) Miriam.

Miriam. I'm sorry Rachel but it's hopeless. At first I thought okay maybe we can make something "wordy" out of it like Mabou Mines or some of that shit they do over at La Mama but when it comes to that rolling on the floor shit, it's like, I don't know, Mel Brooks. I just don't like it.

Rachel. It's not your job to like it, it's your job to act it. Like (*pointing at Anthea*) her commercial.

Miriam. Not this thing.

Rachel. Miriam if you leave again I will never speak to you. Ever.

Miriam. Too bad for you.

Rachel. You stay and do what you promised to do.

Miriam. I didn't promise to do anything.

Rachel. You promised to be in my friend's play.

Miriam. (*Laughing again.*) Yea. I said I'd be in a play. So far I haven't seen one. (*Miriam sits and starts writing her number on a piece of paper.*)

Rachel. (*Holding the script.*) This is the play. You haven't given it a chance to find that out. You haven't given it a chance to express herself. You closed your mind before you heard any of her words.

Miriam. I gave that thing every chance it deserved. I wasted a couple hours of my life giving it a chance. Paper plates and peas and carrots and rolling on the floor of honey. Please.

Rachel. You are truly unbelievable.

Miriam. Here Anthea. Here's my number. Call me when you're ready to tell those yellow stain people to go fuck themselves. You too Emily.

Joanne. Well if Miriam's quitting then so am I.

Rachel. Oh my God.

Joanne. Well Rachel. To be honest, you did say this was the last chance.

Rachel. This is the worst day of my life.

Joanne. Just a minute Rachel, let me get my stuff. You want to meet Eddie. He'll be waiting outside.

Miriam. I'll pass.

Rachel. (*Speaking to anyone who might be listening.*) I just can't believe this. It's like she's dying all over again.

Joanne. Anthea are you and Emily staying?

Anthea. I'm not sure I know what's going on.

Rachel. Miriam don't you dare walk out of here!

Miriam. Or what?

Rachel. Or I'll play it.

Miriam. Play what?

Rachel. You know what.

Miriam. (*Pause. She knows what Rachel's talking about. She moves toward Rachel like she's going to punch her.*) You mean you kept that recording? And you have it with you? Or did you just bring it today so you could blackmail me into being your stupid friend's play?

Rachel. She wasn't stupid! She was disturbed!

Miriam. I'll say.

Rachel. You don't know what a great woman she was. She had a spirit. A real spirit.

Miriam. So what? Come on everyone, the spirit in this place is beginning to stink. I'm being overwhelmed by the smell of the spirit here!

Rachel. No. I have something I want everyone to hear.

Miriam. (*Walking toward Rachel, menacingly.*) Okay. Fine. Play it.

Rachel. I don't want to I just want you to stop being so angry.

Miriam. I'm not angry. I'm honest.

Rachel. You're mean.

Miriam. It's the way I am.

Rachel. It's not the way you were.

Miriam. It's the way I am!

Rachel. Yes to cover up feeling and vulnerabilities.

Miriam. Oh my God. Go ahead. Play your recording. Or no I'll play it. (*Miriam finds Rachel's device and looks at whatever's listed.*) Ahh. Nicely labeled. Rachel Tod and Amy eating lunch and talking about Miriam. (*She plays it.*)

Recording:

Tod. Oh my God. I saw her get in this fight with Stephanie Simmons in Mr. Sawinski's class. I couldn't believe it. Miriam had a whip.

Amy. No way.

Rachel. Oh God.

Tod. Yes and she was cracking it on the floor but not hitting her and then Stephanie picked up a chair and threw it at Miriam, and then they started rolling around on the floor with Miriam on top of Stephanie trying to gouge her eyes out with her thumbs.

Rachel. Oh God.

Tod. Then Mr. Sawinski came running over and
kicked Miriam in the stomach and she was lying
on the floor just screaming 'bastards, bastards.'
Everybody was staring at her. She's so scary.
Who comes to school with a whip?

Amy. Everybody hates her.

Rachel. I don't.

Amy. Why not?

Rachel. I feel sorry for her.

Tod. But she brings it on herself.

Rachel. She has a hard life.

Amy. That doesn't matter. Everyone still hates her.
(*Rachel shuts off the recording.*)

Joanne. What they hell kind of school did you girls go
to?

Rachel. A very bad one.

Anthea. Did that teacher really kick you?

Miriam. Yes. Got him sent to the rubber room.

Anthea. The rubber room?

Miriam. It's where they send the teachers who assault
students, so they don't lose their jobs, you know,
because it's really important that nice family men
who kick girls in the stomach keep their jobs. Well
thanks for the memories Rachel. Still don't know
why you're carrying that shit around; it's been more
than ten years.

Rachel. (*Says this with great 'symbolism'*) I'm not the
one carrying it around.

Miriam. Oh come on! What is it with you? Joanne's
been running in and out of here like this Eddie putz
has got her tied to the end of a yo-yo but I'm the
disruptive one. Right? I'm the one that's causing all

the problems. All those other girls quit because they knew I was about to come through the door. I'm not bitter Rachel. I'm real. And that doesn't come from pain.

Rachel. I was there.

Miriam. (*Pauses.*) Fuck. You. You stupid bitch.

Rachel. Fine! That's the way you want to play, I'll play. Everyone, there's a story you should know about Miriam. It's called "Mr. Potato Head."

Miriam. You tell that story and I'll fucking kill you.

Rachel. I wish I had dime for every time you said you were going to kill me. I could hire professional actors. I don't want to tell this story.

Miriam. Then don't.

Rachel. Then stay.

Miriam. I can't. It's stupid. I can't do it.

Rachel. It's not. It's beautiful and poetic and just because you can't see that yet...

Miriam. It's bullshit.

Rachel. It's not. And anyway we're not talking about the play right now we're talking about your...

Miriam. (*Talking over Rachel.*) That's right because every time I offend you, you start talking about something that happened twenty years ago.

Rachel. ...inability to face...

(*At some point during Rachel and Miriam's argument, Emily quietly moves to retrieve her things. She calmly picks them up and starts to leave. Rachel notices before she goes.*)

Rachel. Emily? Where are you going?

Emily. I'm leaving.

Rachel. You can't leave.

Emily. That's where you're wrong. I suddenly realized that I can.

Rachel. But...

Emily. I can't listen to this anymore. Not one more second. I'll probably explode if I try to stay.

Rachel. Emily?

Emily. You're a bunch of liars anyway. So am I.

Rachel. Why would you say such a thing?

Emily. You're standing there screaming at Miriam just to avoid admitting that this is a terrible play. Miriam's quit. Joanne's quit. I'm quitting too. I'm sorry.

Rachel. Emily please. Not now.

Emily. (*Leaving.*) Goodbye Rachel.

Rachel. You can't.

Emily. (*Stops.*) Oh Rachel look. I've been scared to say anything but I know the reason you're so desperate to do this play — this particular play — is because she killed herself right? The woman you admired so much? Looked up to? She killed herself right? And you're miserable because you don't know why and you'd rather pretend that this is a good play written by an undiscovered genius instead of an incomprehensible mess written by a damaged person.

Rachel. (*Angry.*) How did you know?

Emily. I just knew. It wasn't hard to figure out.

Rachel. You went into my things didn't you? You found the note she left me.

Emily. I would never that do. How can you accuse me of that?

Rachel. I'm sorry it's just I don't understand how you knew.

Emily. (*Loudly*) So you accuse me of sneaking into your purse?

Rachel. Well don't get upset I just don't understand

how you knew.

Emily. I knew because I've watched you try to cover it up for the last four weeks. (*Pause.*) And then Shelly told me. Well I mean she confirmed it.

Rachel. She told you?

Emily. She confirmed it. I told you I already knew.

Rachel. Well don't be mad.

Emily. I'm very mad.

Rachel. This isn't like you.

Emily. No. It's not.

Rachel. Well what's the matter? (*Pause.*) What?

Emily. You didn't even ask me.

Rachel. Ask you what?

Emily. If I wanted to change parts. If I would mind playing The Silent One.

Rachel. Yes I did.

Emily. You didn't.

Rachel. I did.

Anthea. No. You didn't.

Rachel. I'm sorry. I guess I just assumed you'd agree.

Emily. Yes because I've always agreed with everybody. I've always gone along with everything.

Rachel. We can switch back.

Emily. No we won't.

Rachel. You mean you want to play The Silent One.

Emily. No. I mean I'm not going to be in the play. I should have left the first day. I suppose I felt I had to do it because it was a noble gesture on your part. I don't know why I couldn't say anything. Maybe Miriam changed it.

Rachel. This is the worst day of my life.

Emily. No it's not. Finding your friend in the bathtub was the worst day of your life. And you aren't doing her any favors by producing a play that doesn't make sense.

Rachel. Emily please stop talking about this.

Emily. No.

Rachel. Yes! I mean. I can't accept it. I just can't. I cared about her so much. I gave her everything I could give. And she accepted what I gave her. Not like Miriam who's never accepted anything I've tried to...

Emily. Miriam does need that. That's obvious don't you think? I mean I try to give people all this niceness and what happens? I get switched from a part with three lines to a part with none. I think Miriam's right. Being nice just because girls are supposed to be nice... well the whole thing is a pile of shit.

Anthea. Oh my.

Joanne. Emily I'm so thrilled to hear you say that.

Emily. "Peace and Love" has problems. But no one can say you didn't care about your friend if you decide not to produce it. You know you loved her. That's what matters. But just because I love all of you doesn't mean I'm obliged to stay and read three lines that I don't even understand. Because I think I know what matters to me.

(*Long pause.*)

Joanne. Well I'm totally confused. First we're having a nice pleasant rehearsal and suddenly Miriam and Rachel are screaming at each other about high school and Emily's using words like shit and damn. I don't get it.

Rachel. Never mind Joanne.

Miriam. Now never mind? (*Miriam stares at Rachel.*) They know just about everything anyway.

Rachel. They don't have to know everything. I should never have said anything.

68

Miriam. You didn't.

Joanne. Well I'm going next door for more coffee.

Rachel. Joanne. If you leave this room one more time which we all know you do just so you can fight with Eddie or tease him or whatever this thing is between you, then you are fired. (*Pause.*) Well as fired as you can be at this point.

Miriam. Sit down Joanne.

Joanne. Why?

Miriam. Just sit down and shut the fuck up. (*Miriam sighs deeply as Joanne sits.*) There's nothing in this world that bothers me except one thing that Rachel happened to see. She was there. See? We go back a long way. And it scarred her for life apparently. And it scarred me for life because it scarred her. She never stops trying to fix me. (*Miriam looks at Rachel but Rachel looks away.*) She can't forget it. And it's stupid. It's just plain stupid.

Joanne. Well I'm about fall down in a heap if you don't tell us. All these Anthea like thoughts are whizzing through my brain like "what if she was raised in a well?" or "what if they slit her feet and made her walk on salt?"

Anthea. Oh no. That would hurt.

Miriam. Raised in a well?

Joanne. Miriam I love you like a sister, even though I don't know you, and I'm worried.

Miriam. Joanne, you're an ass. Rachel was a new kid and she seemed nice so I brought her home after school when I knew my mother would be passed out drinking. Her 6 o'clock glass of Ernest and Julio Gallo usually started around noon and then... Well she used to have us bury the bottles in the back yard because she thought *(air quotes)* "no one would know." And she had about 6 or 7 different liquor stores outside the Chicago area that she hit up once a week. Sundays she didn't drink. That was Blue Day cause of the Blue laws. That's what always "proved" in her mind that she could control it cause Sunday was always a nice drug free day.

Anthea. I thought you said wine?

Miriam. Alcohol's a drug. Anyway I brought Rachel over; showed her my house; showed her my toys; showed the door to my mother's bedroom and told her not to wake her. I had this Thumbellina doll.

Anthea. Oh you had a little Thumbellina?

Miriam. No Anthea. I had a lightbulb to play with. That's what she gave me. A lightbulb.

Anthea. (*quietly but loud enough*) Oh what a wit.

Miriam. (*Raising her hands in surrender.*) You're right. Sorry. Anyway I kept Thumbellina in a dresser because my mother didn't know I had it. This Thumbellina kid was like my best friend. I don't know. We were really young. If my mother beat me I'd run to my room and hide there in the closet with this doll and I made up all sorts of stories about evil creatures like witches and devils and ghouls and monsters — except they were all good and friendly ones — like pals — and they would come to rescue me and Thumbellina and devour my mother, usually by eating her alive. When I got older of course I realized the booze was eating her alive, but I was really young. And I never imagined like, "good fairies," or "fairy godmothers," or any of those nice pretty chicks to come along and wave a wand and save me. It was always monsters and zombies and Halloween creatures with me. So I showed Rachel my Thumbellina doll and...

70

Anthea. What was her name?

Miriam. Theena. Theena Thumbellina. Anyway I
showed Rachel my doll and we were playing in the
living room but then Theena said she wanted to
watch. So I set her on top of my mom's upright
piano that she never played — inherited it or
something — and then I heard my mother's car door
slam. And I went like, into a panic or something. I
don't remember it well. I thought she was in the
bedroom sleeping it off. But she must have run out
that day, or gone through the two bottles already,
and she comes stumbling in, and the thing is she had
run over some little kids dog and killed it. That's
how bad she was. I mean this woman was like an
axe with legs.

Rachel. (*Rachel laughs, but no one else does.*) More
like a guillotine.

Miriam. She sees Theena sitting there on the piano and
starts screaming her head off. Apparently no one
was allowed to touch her dear dead mother's piano.
Rachel just backs up into a corner and crouched
behind the couch, scared out of her mind cause she
ain't seen anything like a raging drunk. And we
were only six or something. But the stupid thing is
she wasn't screaming, "What's Thumbellina doing
on my piano!" She was screaming, "What's Mr.
Potato Head doing on my piano!" And inside I'm
thinking "She's Thumbellina," but I couldn't say
anything because the only way I could get my
mother to stop her rages is if I got on my knees and
held onto her ankles. So that's what I did. But she
didn't pity me. I was crying, "Mommy don't start,"
and she was just screaming her head off about this
potato on her piano. And I tried to change the

71

subject and said, "My friends here. Rachel's here," but she just screamed "I don't want to meet no fucking friend. Get this fucking potato off my piano!" And I'm just like, "Her name is Theena. She's a Thumbellina. Her name is Theena. She's my friend." And then my mother goes into the kitchen, grabs a big old meat cleaver. She grabs Theena, puts her on the floor, raised the knife way up in the air and then "thwack," totally decapitates my doll. And I start screaming and... I don't know... somehow it became real... and my imagination just... I don't know. A six year old imagination just... you fill in the blanks. Stuff that isn't really anything just seems like a nightmare. I could see blood gushing out of my doll's body and I kept trying to put her head back on. She had killed her. My mother killed my doll. I don't remember what happened to Rachel or anything after that.

Rachel. I was scared out of my mind. I had never seen any grown up person act that way. I ran from the house. But I wanted to hug you. I've always wanted us to process this together...

Miriam. (*Shushing her in a nice way, like with a couple of fingers on her lips.*) I'm only going to say this one more time. And if you don't hear me this time then we we'll leave here and never see each other again. Ever. And I mean it. I don't. Want. Your pity. You knew all through school what I went home to, and I appreciated the fact that you didn't tell anyone. And then finally that woman ended up in the hospital with liver failure and that was it. I didn't even visit until I had to identify the body. But I didn't want your pity then and I never wanted your pity. If anything, I just wanted your silence. And you gave it to me. That's what you never understood. You gave me what I wanted.

Rachel. Friendship. It was never pity Miriam. It was just friendship.

Miriam. Then why does it always feel like pity? Pity makes it unequal. Friendship is equal.

Rachel. I don't know.

Anthea. Well I pity you. And I don't care if you don't like it.

Joanne. Well I have a confession to make too.

Anthea. Oh honey. Can't this wait? I'm exhausted and I've got a diaper commercial to do next week.

Emily. You're going to do it?

Anthea. Yes. Take anything that comes your way. Do anything except what your moral compass tells you you can't do. That's the actor's plight.

Joanne. No everybody, listen. I want to say something too.

Rachel. Joanne, I'm begging you, not now.

Joanne. (*Throwing her arms up in the air and acting like this is a surprise announcement.*) I love that man. I don't know why. He follows me around like a fish on a leash but he does everything I want. The other day we went shoplifting like they did in *Breakfast At Tiffany's*. Even our sex is great. Like this one night we were going at it and I noticed this big rubber band next to the bed so I took it and lowered over his big fat...

Rachel. I don't want to hear this!

Joanne. But I haven't finished.

Rachel. We get the gist.

Joanne. It's just one word. One big huge word.

Rachel. No! Yuck! Gross! I take it we're not doing this play anymore. In fact — this is so hard to say — I don't want to do this play. But I would still like to do something as a tribute. She was still my... friend. It scares me but I have a play of my which I finished recently. Last night in fact. It's five parts. Five women. One of which I can play myself. Just one act. Would you all consider reading it for me? We won't attempt a production, we'll just do a free script in hand reading and invite everyone we know. People love that stuff.

Miriam. No they don't.

Rachel. Well — they'll come anyway. That's what New York theatre is all about anyway. Just trying different things and seeing if your friends can pretend to like it.

Anthea. Well of course I will.

Rachel. Emily?

Emily. Would I have more than there lines?

Rachel. You'd have hundreds of lines.

Emily. Okay.

Joanne. Joanne?

Joanne. I guess so. COCK! And he came buckets!

Rachel. (*She shivers.*) Uck. Miriam.

Miriam. Why do I do this? I don't know. It's work I guess. I'm not making any promises.

Rachel. Neither am I.

Miriam. Fair enough.

Rachel. (*Quietly to Miriam, who looks away.*) I'm sorry.

Miriam. No checks, bare feet or apologies accepted.

Rachel. I take it back. No apologies. But do you feel okay?

Miriam. Ehh. I got a headache and my butt hurts. (*She looks at Rachel.*) Ahh you stupid shit get over here. (*Rachel goes to Miriam and they hug. When they're done, Rachel — perhaps crying and more moved by this than Miriam — turns around, straightens her clothing, then crosses to her bag and pulls out five copies of her script.*)

Rachel. Okay. Here are five copies of my play.

Emily. You just happened to bring five copies of your own play?

Rachel. I have no comment. Since it's just a first reading I think we should sit in a circle and react to each other. We'll try to have a conversational level reality and nothing more. No blocking or major interpretation. Okay? (*The five move to their chairs in a horseshoe shape. Emily is in the front on the right side.*)

Rachel. Emily you'll like this one, or you'll like your part I think. You end the play.

Emily. I end it?

Rachel. You're sort of my alter ego in the play and I give you the last things to say. Look at the end.

Emily (*She begins reading in the chair, bent over the script.*) We read Rachel's play — and it was a play and we enjoyed it and we decided to do it. Miriam took us out later that day. First we all went over to Anthea's apartment and helped her practice for her commercial. It's amazing how many ways you can say the phrase, "Just like me." That was her only line. After extolling all the benefits of adult diapers for incontinent people, the commercial inserted a montage of five or six "ordinary people" saying, "like me," or "just like me." It was a stigma reduction commercial. One of the first of its kind. (*Emily put the script down and turns directly to the audience. The others all freeze in their chairs.*) We hung out talking and drinking beer. And later we piled into a large cab and told the driver to take us down Fifth Avenue. Miriam wanted to scream things at strangers. It seemed to be one of her past times. Joanne volunteered to go first, stuck her head out the window and screamed at the cab behind us.

Joanne. Quit following me Eddie!

Emily. Then Anthea it was your turn and you shouted at a tourist.

Anthea. I think you're a fat jerk and I'm sorry for saying that; I don't really mean it.

Emily. And quickly pulled your head back in the car. And then Rachel you screamed.

Rachel. The honey of truth is often a bitter spread. (*Rachel shakes her head.*) God what is wrong with me?

Emily. And then Miriam.

Rachel. Mrs. Potato Head's on the piano because she's watching me have a good time! (*To the others.*) Notice I called her Mrs. Potato Head. That's feminism in action.

Emily. And then it was my turn and wimpy old me all I could say was, "I like your dress." Aghh. What's wrong with me? Why do I always have to be nice? What does anyone know? Why we were there? Why we had come together to make a play? Miriam took us to one of those large dance clubs with a really long line at the side of the building to get in — I think it was called The Tunnel. I had never been to a club like that and Anthea was practically petrified — but Miriam took us to the front of the line and said a few things to the bouncer who she seemed to know and he let us in ahead of everyone. And we danced and drank and met men, who were jerks, but we met them anyway. And then we kind of got lost in the crowd — each of us sort of... moving on in her own way. The last time I saw Rachel, she was leaning against the bar and seemed to have taken a very keen interest in this dark haired and muscular woman who had an odd resemblance to Miriam. I think we all knew, even before that, what her propensity was. She just wasn't ready at that point in her life to make it public. Eddie, who had followed us in the cab, eventually got admitted to the club by waiting in line and the last time I saw Joanne, she and he were making out in some big stuffed chair. Miriam ran into a guy she seemed to know from somewhere else, who was blonde, sort of thin, wore round glasses and looked kind of like a professor in one of those Ivy League colleges. Totally not the type I would have thought for her. They went off somewhere; disappeared into the night. And then it was just Anthea and me dancing together, like two little hangers-on; like that character in *West Side Story* they nicknamed Anybody's or Nobody's cause they didn't care which gang she belonged to.

I think we were feeling alone and awkward, and Anthea shouted in my ear that she was going to get another beer, but she never returned. She just sort of disappeared into the mystery of the future. And then I was dancing with myself. Like Billy Idol. But I didn't feel awkward and one of the great things about New York, it seems to me, is that because no one notices you, you have a kind of freedom that you rarely find elsewhere. A freedom from the great trap of gossip. And then an Aretha Franklin song came on and it just lifted my spirits because I realized, in that song, that we can be happy in our struggles. And somehow that put it all together. I

went home by myself and woke up with a splitting headache. The worst of my life. I went to my economy sized bottled of aspirin and stood there in the bathroom with the bottle in my hands, looking at my naked body, my small upturned breasts, that small pooch in the lower stomach that most women get. What is the name of that thing? Pelvic tilt or something. But I looked at this woman that was supposed to be me, and wondered if I had a personality, or if I was just going to be nice all my life – if, when challenged to shout something at a random person on the street all I will ever be able to say is, "I like your dress."
(*Somewhere around here, Aretha Franklin's Another Night, starts quietly.*)
With that massive rum and coke headache and strains of Ms. Franklin still ringing in my ears, I decided there was a me somewhere underneath all this niceness, and I did the strangest thing. I flushed all my aspirin down the toilet. After all these years of doing things for the polite reasons, or the nice reasons, I didn't want to lose the remnant — the hangover — of having done something for the right reason. And I have to say, it was the best hangover I've ever had.

(*She laughs as the lights go down quickly and the music soars and that is...*)

The End

www.ingramcontent.com/pod-product-compliance
Lightning Source LLC
Chambersburg PA
CBHW021210020426
42331CB00003B/300